a civil war
without guns

20 YEARS ON
the lessons of the 1984-85 miners' strike

a civil war
without guns

20 YEARS ON
the lessons of the 1984-85 miners' strike

by ken smith

Socialist Publications
May 2004

A Civil War without Guns
20 Years On - The Lessons of the 1984-85 Miners' Strike
by Ken Smith
© Socialist Publications 2004

First Edition April 2004
Reprinted March 2009
Classification: Politics / History
Ken Smith
A Civil War without Guns - the 1984-85 Miners' Strike

ISBN 978-1-870958-46-2

Published by Socialist Publications
for the Socialist Party
Typeset by Kavita Graphics
Typeset in Utopia 9 pt

Distribution by Socialist Books
PO Box 24697, London, E11 1YD
Telephone +44 (0)20 8988 8777

design & layout: Kavita Graphics +44 (0)20 7252 1915
e-mail: dennis@kavitagraphics.co.uk

cover photograph: Orgreave, 18 June 1984. Lesley Boulton from the Sheffield miners' support group shouts for an ambulance for an injured miner. A mounted policeman swears at her and hits out with his truncheon and she can only raise her hand for protection. credit: John Harris

a civil war without guns

20 YEARS ON

the lessons of the 1984-85 miners' strike

by ken smith

Acknowledgements

There is a need to rescue the many heroic endeavors of the millions of ordinary working-class people and especially of the miners and their families that were carried out during the strike.

In much of the material that has been broadcast or written to mark the 20th anniversary of the strike their struggle has at best been portrayed as a brave but tragic attempt to save a dying industry.

No matter how sympathetically the miners, their families and their supporters may be viewed that portrayal does a massive disservice to the momentous struggle they conducted. It is absolutely vital for the struggles of future generations of trade unionists and socialist militants that a more instructive balance sheet of the strike is given.

It is to these ordinary self-sacrificing workers, who should never be forgotten by future generations, that this account is dedicated. I encountered and worked alongside hundreds – if not thousands – of these comrades during the strike itself in South Wales and throughout Britain.

I could not name all of those miners and their families and my comrades in Militant and the Socialist Party who have inspired and helped me to write this account.

But, particularly I would acknowledge the Militant miners of St John's colliery in Maesteg, South Wales, who I worked alongside during the strike. These included people like Ian Isaac, Philip White, Billy Pye, Bobby Potts, Peter Clements, Paul Davies, the late Charlie White, Ron Roberts, Colin Schofield, Ieuan Dare, Rob Bevan, Rob James, Derek Williams and others – the miners' wives and their active supporters, like Vi John, Eirlys Furlong, Teresa Parry, Lynda Sullivan, Linda Williams, Shirley Wells, Jan Dare, Karin Clements, Idwal Isaac and many others will always hold my special affection, regardless of how little contact we have had since and how divergent our political paths have become.

And, I would like to thank comrades from Militant, as it was in 1984, and Socialist Party members who have given political assistance and advice in going back over the events of 1984-85.

In particular, Peter Taaffe, Socialist Party general secretary, encouraged me to write this account and has given many valuable comments. Alec Thraves, the Socialist Party Wales secretary, was always a great assistance and encouragement in 1984-85 and has been on many occasions since. He has also assisted by reading this book and making many important points.

Ian Isaac met up with me a couple of times and read parts of the manuscript and provided excellent factual information, constructive comments and vital background material.

Others who read the manuscript in various drafts and gave invaluable assistance and comments include: Bill Mullins, Hannah Sell, Jane James, Dave Griffiths, Jon Dale, Steve Minney and Bob Sulatycki.

Roger Shrives, Alison Hill and Manny Thain all proofread the book at various stages and Alison Hill also did the picture research.

Andrew Glyn provided essential material, particularly on the economics of pit closures. Alan Hardman's cartoons are still as hard hitting about the strike in 2004 as they were in 1984 and many thanks to Alan for allowing them to be used.

Finally thanks and appreciation go to my family for putting up with me while writing this book – especially my partner Jane and my daughter Nanci, who I hope will one day read this material and understand what it is that inspires her dad to have fought alongside the miners and others for a better, socialist world.

Ken Smith - April 2004

About the author

Ken Smith is a member of the Socialist Party executive committee. He has been involved in socialist politics since the mid-1970s in South Wales and London.

During the 1984-85 miners' strike he was an organiser for Militant (forerunner of the Socialist Party) in South Wales.

Early on in the strike he was elected the chair of the Llynfi and Afan Valley Miners' Support Group. The group worked closely alongside St John's NUM Lodge and other lodges in the two valleys to organise the political and financial support for nearly a thousand miners and their families during the strike.

About the cartoonist

Alan Hardman has been drawing excellent cartoons and illustrations for the Militant, Militant International Review, the Socialist and Socialism Today since the early 1970s. His work has also been used in many labour movement publications internationally.

During the miners' strike Alan's work gave tremendous inspiration to all those involved in the struggle. Many of his cartoons were also used by NUM branches and miners' support group on their leaflets, posters and publications.

To this day the cartoons retain a sharpness in conveying the issues surrounding the strike, bringing it once more to life for those who lived through it and for those discovering it for the first time.

Introduction

TWENTY YEARS ago British miners were forced into strike action to defend their jobs, their communities and their way of life. The strike became a trial of strength between Thatcher's Tory government and the miners that still reverberates throughout the workers' movement and society.

The strike, as former Labour MP and political commentator Brian Walden remarked at the time, "was a civil war without guns"; a battle between the workers and the ruling class.

Although guns were not used against strikers the whole panoply of the state forces, including weapons, cavalry, spies and the courts were used to try and intimidate the miners back to work. They held out for a year in the most determined show of strength; stiffened up by the magnificent solidarity of the working class in Britain and internationally.

That the miners were ultimately defeated was not down to their lack of courage or determination, nor the support shown them by the working class. Thatcher and the ruling class ultimately won but not through their own strength. Instead it was the right wing leaders of the trade unions and the Labour Party who stabbed the miners in the back and led to the social and economic devastation of the mining communities.

The strike's defeat was a bitter blow for those miners and their families who struggled. Their betrayal by the right-wing Labour and union leaders meant that their jobs were to disappear forever and their communities turned into industrial wastelands.

A report in the *Observer* outlined what it has meant for one of the biggest former mining communities in Britain: *"Barnsley has suffered all the classic depressive symptoms of a northern industrial town: unemployment, drug abuse and crime at some of the highest levels in the country.*

"Until the 1980s, one in five of all Barnsley men worked in the mines. Now the figure is zero. Anne Lewis of the Child and Adolescent Mental Health Service said the closure of the mines had a devastating effect on the town's youth. Barnsley became an area of huge deprivation. Some 42% of Barnsley's children now live in poverty." [1]

The miners' defeat, along with the economic upswing of the late 1980s, ushered in a complex and difficult period in Britain, which consolidated a shift to the right at the top of the labour movement that had started in 1981 but had been cut across by the year-long strike. Thereafter, Labour and trade union leaders abandoned any pretence of struggle against Thatcherite industrial run-down and privatisation and meekly accepted anti-union legislation.

Following on from the miners' strike, the collapse of the Stalinist states of the former Soviet Union and eastern Europe and the subsequent ideological offensive of the capitalist ruling class internationally greatly reinforced these trends. The leaders of the workers' organisations used the miners' defeat and the collapse of Stalinism to argue that class struggle was outdated and that there was no ideological or practical alternative to the capitalist market.

The end of class politics?

THE VICTORS of the miners' dispute and their apologists in the labour movement have always attempted to portray the strike as an ideologically doomed, futile attempt by one man – Arthur Scargill - to preserve a dying industry.

Michael Ignatieff, regarded as something of a cultural guru by the ruling class in the 1980s but little remembered now, wrote in the New Statesman towards the end of the strike that *"the miners' strike is not the vindication of class politics but its death throes."* [2]

The Labour Party tops at the time of the strike, like leader Neil Kinnock and his deputy Roy Hattersley have also tried to boil the strike down to the character and tactical 'ineptness' of Arthur Scargill. (These people were themselves such master tacticians that they squandered a 5% opinion poll lead at the time of the miners' strike to lose the 1987 general election. Learning nothing from that, their tactical adroitness allowed them to go on to lose the 1992 general election as well).

Neil Kinnock, denounced at the time by Labour MP Bob Parry as one of the greatest traitors in labour movement history, used his betrayal of the miners and the attacks he conducted against Liverpool city council in the 1980s, as a stepping stone to the millionaire lifestyle he now enjoys as a European Commissioner. To him, 20 years on, it was simple: *"The tragedy is that there was no mandate for the strike. The fault has to lie with Scargill."* [3]

Hattersley, whilst giving more credit to Scargill for correctly defending the mining communities, still said the miners' defeat was simply down to the NUM president not calling a ballot. And, according to Hattersley, the 'best' outcome of a miners' ballot during the strike would have been that *"The victory would not have been complete, The unstoppable advance of the global market would have made pit closures inevitable and the balance sheet of profit and loss would have guaranteed an accelerating decline."* [4]

What seems to have escaped Kinnock and Hattersley's notice, however, is that before the miners began their action, the Tories had massacred jobs across British industry.

Steelworkers had embarked on a 13-week strike in 1980 after a ballot but - because their leaders crumbled before the Tories - over 80,000 jobs were lost in British Steel within three years.

From Thatcher's election in 1979 to the start of the miners' strike, 1,600 jobs were lost every week in Britain with hardly a squeak of resistance from some union leaders. Even in the coal industry, where miners had shown themselves prepared to fight, over 100 jobs were lost every week as unemployment soared to over three million.

From the Tory general election victory of 1979 onwards, prime minister Margaret Thatcher had been gauging the temper of the British working class and in particular the willingness of the trade union and Labour leaders to struggle against the social counter-revolution she was embarking upon.

Before the miners' strike there had been a number of occasions where the proclaimed defiance of the union leaders against everything Thatcher stood for had proved to be rhetoric: such as attacks on trade unionism in the car industry, the defeat of the 13-week long steel strike in 1980 and the union leaders' inability to deliver the threat of general strike action when the anti-union laws were first used against the print workers' union from late 1983 to early 1984.

But, all of these were only partial stages in Thatcher's plan to weaken or destroy the power of the workers' organisations, which stood in the way of her carrying through a shift in the balance of power in favour of the bosses.

Learning from defeat

THERE HAVE been millions of words written about the strike. However, there are still many issues that a new generation of trade unionists and socialists need to discuss today.

Some on the Left have simplistically concluded that either the strike showed that the Tory government and state forces were too strong to be taken on and defeated, or that all that was needed, in the fashion of first world war generals, was to throw more troops out of the trenches.

Neither answer is adequate. But was there any way the miners could have won this massive defensive battle and avoided the Thatcherite scorched earth policy which reduced former manufacturing areas to wastelands?

The answer is undoubtedly yes. They could have won if the trade union leaders had shown the same commitment in action to supporting the miners as the rank and file of their unions did.

More than ever, a proper accounting of the strike and its aftermath is necessary to strip away the one-sided pessimistic gloss heavily applied throughout the years.

There is a need to rescue the heroic endeavours during the strike of the millions of ordinary working-class people - especially the miners and their families. In what were posed as insurmountable odds, even by many union leaders, it needs to be recalled how close the miners and their supporters actually came to achieving a historic victory, which would have raised the whole of the working class a head taller.

But to answer how the miners could have won, many complex questions thrown up by the strike need to be seriously addressed: Was the strike inevitable? Did the miners and NUM leaders have any other options? Should they have had a ballot ? Was mass picketing successfully carried out?

If the strategy and tactics of the miners' leaders had been different could they have secured a victory and what would the impact of that have been?

Had the miners won then the immediate history following the strike would have been radically different. Thatcher and her government would have been massively discredited and it probably would have led to her resignation. Although we should never underestimate the ineptitude of the then Labour leader Neil Kinnock in snatching defeat from the jaws of victory, it would have been likely that a Labour government would have come to power.

The pit-closure plan would have been initially dropped. But at a certain stage the miners would have once again needed to fight for their industry and for the removal of the rigged Tory market in energy along with advocating a socialist plan of production for the mining and energy industries.

Lastly, under pressure from a confident working class, even a Kinnock Labour government would have had to carry through some measures in favour of the working class, perhaps being compelled to abolish the Tory anti-union laws. One of Kinnock's principal reasons for his attacks on the miners was his fear of a rising tide of militancy in the event of a miners' victory - he didn't want to see militancy pay, especially not if he were to become prime minister.

Struggle historically justified

WHATEVER THE background and outcome to their struggle the miners had no option but to fight in 1984. The fact that they fought so valiantly against the subsequent rundown of their industry shows they were right to struggle in the way they did under Arthur Scargill.

Had the miners not done so then the Tory pit-closure programme would have proceeded much more rapidly and many other anti-working class measures would have been introduced earlier than they were.

Their stand has been historically vindicated. Amongst the miners and the general public, particularly after the Tories' second wave of pit closures was announced in 1992 against a huge public outcry, there was an overwhelming recognition that they were right to fight.

The miners' strike also politicised a generation of young people and at the time produced a massive shift to the left on many issues in society. It inspired, for example, the quarter of a million-strong national school student strike, called by Militant supporters, which followed within months of the end of the strike.

Most importantly the miners' strike showed the willingness of working-class people to struggle to change society.

New militancy

THE 'OFFICIAL' right-wing view of the strike as a 'terrible defeat' has been held over the head of trade unionists, socialists and left-wing organisations like the sword of Damocles for the last 20 years. But after 20 years there are signs of a new militancy amongst workers, witnessed in the firefighters, postal and Heathrow baggage handlers' disputes of 2003.

There has been, despite the retirement of Arthur Scargill, talk of the re-emergence of 'Scargillism' – it was one of the first lines of attack against the firefighters in their dispute. It was not a label that fitted well on their national leaders: especially not their 'moderate' general secretary, Andy Gilchrist.

However, a new generation of workers, trade unionists and socialists should now take the opportunity to re-examine the events and lessons of the strike to ensure they are better equipped to win their own industrial battles and succeed in the socialist struggle to change society.

Although there is a detailed chronology of the main events and bibliography of books giving very detailed accounts of the strike included, this account does not intend to chronologically chart all the developments in the strike. Instead the aim is to bring out general lessons which can help the Left in the trade unions today. (Many of the specific examples I give are from South Wales where I lived and worked alongside miners and their wives in 1984 but hopefully the reader will see they are used to illustrate general processes at work).

In particular, this account intends to show that Britain during this colossal battle was involved in a virtual civil war with the working class solidly behind the miners and – particularly when she was winning – the ruling class solidly behind Thatcher.

We never believed that the miners' defeat was preordained as some on the Left felt – including the Socialist Workers' Party with its theory of the 'downturn' which ultimately held that workers' struggles could not be successful.

And a recounting of that momentous year holds many rich lessons for future struggles of working-class people, which need to be touched on. In particular it should address key questions that have been used since the strike to hold back workers' struggles by the right-wing union leaders.

They have used the strike's defeat as a means to attack militancy and justify their rolling over in front of the bosses' attacks, which has led to a big reduction in union membership that is only now beginning to be reversed.

Although the new generation of union members have shown little fear of the anti-union laws as they have moved into struggle, the new Left leaders in the trade unions, the so-called 'awkward squad', are still intimidated by the miners' defeat. The awkward squad have (so far) lacked confidence to launch the kind of all-out struggles needed which could successfully turn the tables on 20 years of the bosses' brutal attacks.

For all of these reasons, and because of the huge volume of material that has denigrated the miners or drawn false and negative conclusions about the strike, there is a need for this account. We hope it will draw out the vital lessons that are applicable to a new generation of working-class militants in the 21st century.

NOTES

1 *Observer*, 22 February 2004

2 *New Statesman*, 14 December 1984

3 *The Independent*, 5 March 2004

4 *The Guardian*, 8 March 2004

List of abbreviations used in this book

Trade Unions

- **NUM** — National Union of Mineworkers
- **NACODS** — National Association of Colliery Overmen, Deputies and Shotfirers
- **COSA** — Colliery Officials Staff Area
- **TUC** — Trades Union Congress
- **NGA** — National Graphical Association
- **TGWU** — Transport and General Workers' Union
- **ISTC** — Iron and Steel Trades Confederation
- **EEPTU** — Electrical, Engineering, Plumbers and Technicians Union
- **NUR** — National Union of Raliwaymen
- **AEU** — Amalgamated Engineering Union
- **CPSA** — Civil and Public Services Association
- **BLOC** — Broad Left Organising Committee

Political organisations

- **LPYS** — Labour Party Young Socialists
- **CP** — Communist Party
- **SWP** — Socialist Workers' Party
- **MP** — Member of Parliament

Industrial organisations

- **NCB** — National Coal Board
- **BSC** — British Steel Coporation
- **ACAS** — Advisory, Conciliation and Arbitration Service

Other organisations

- **MI5** — The name given to Britain's internal secret service
- **MI6** — The name of Britain's external/foreign secret service
- **GCHQ** — The government's surveillance centre at Cheltenham

Chronology

The events of the 1984-85 miners' strike

1983
- **1 September** Ian MacGregor takes over as NCB chairman
- **27 September** NUM submits annual pay claim
- **29 September** NCB turns down pay claim
- **21 October** Special NUM delegate conference votes for overtime ban against pit closures and 5.2% pay offer
- **31 October** Start of national overtime ban
- **November** NCB confirms 49 pits will close due to 'exhausted reserves'

1984
- **23 January** NCB says 19,000 sent home due to overtime ban. Many local disputes ensue
- **20 February** Scottish NUM leaders reject call for all-out strike over threatened closures in Scotland, although backing given to Polmaise strike
- **1 March** Closure of Cortonwood pit announced, with five years' production still to go. 55,000 Yorkshire miners called out on strike under Rule 41 from a ballot result in 1981
- **5 March** Yorkshire NUM calls total stoppage from 12 March
- **6 March** Scottish area NUM calls strike from 9 March. NCB announces cutback of another four million tonnes coal production
- **8 March** NUM national executive declares strikes in Yorkshire and Scotland official, and any other area 'which takes similar action'
- **12 March** Strike solid in Yorkshire, Kent, South Wales and Scotland
- **14 March** NCB obtains High Court injunction instructing Yorkshire NUM to call off pickets. It is ignored

  Police drafted in to mining areas from 21 of the 43 police forces in Britain
- **15 March** David Jones, aged 24, killed at Ollerton, while picketing. Notts area leaders call Notts miners out
- **18 March** Massive police operation starts. Up to 8,000 police are sent to the Nottingham coalfield
- **19 March** Sections of Notts miners say they will carry on working
- **20 March** Kent miners lose legal action against police roadblocks at Dartford Tunnel
- **22 March** Power union leaders advise members to cross picket lines
- **23 March** Police seal off all of Nottinghamshire

● **26 March**   NUM leaders tell right-wing TUC leaders to stay out of the strike

NACODS vote to accept pay offer

● **27 March**   Secret gathering of right-wing NUM leaders issue call through media for a national ballot, end of flying pickets and return to work

● **3 April**   National Union of Railwaymen tells members to block movements of coal

First soup kitchens open in the coalfields

● **11 April**   NACODS vote by 7,638 to 6,661 in favour of strike but this does not reach the union's required two-thirds majority

● **12 April**   Labour leader Neil Kinnock calls for a national ballot

● **19 April**   NUM special delegate conference supports action in all British coalfields. Resolutions for a ballot overwhelmingly rejected

● **1 May**   Notts miners given day off by NCB to demonstrate against strike outside Notts NUM area headquarters

● **2 May**   Number of arrests reaches 1,479

Mass picket of Haworth colliery – up to 10,000-strong

● **3 May**   British Steel starts bringing coal into steel plants with scab lorries

● **8 May**   Coke supplies for Llanwern guaranteed by South Wales NUM

● **11 May**   Scottish area NUM agrees coal trains supplying Ravenscraig to resume

● **12 May**   10,000 women on Women Against Pit Closures demonstration in Barnsley

● **14 May**   Rally in Mansfield of up to 40,000 striking miners and supporters. Police attack demonstrators in car park and arrest 56 on riot charges and five for conspiracy

● **16 May**   Anne Scargill, wife of the NUM president, arrested on picket line

● **17 May**   Tory Home Secretary Leon Brittan admits in Parliament that plain-clothes police are operating in the Nottinghamshire coalfield

● **20 May**   TUC general secretary Len Murray declares "unconstitutional" one-day general strikes in support of miners in Yorkshire, Humberside and South Wales

● **23 May**   NUM leaders meet MacGregor and NCB for talks, which collapse the same day

● **25 May**   High Court instructs NUM not to discipline Notts miners. Convoys of lorries carrying coking coal start from Orgreave coke depot to Scunthorpe steelworks

● **26-28 May**   Orgreave pickets begin to swell in numbers

● **29 May**   Mass picket of 7,000-plus at Orgreave. Riot police deployed for the first time. 82 arrests, 69 injured

● **30 May**   Arthur Scargill arrested at Orgreave. Massive mounted police operation

● **1 June**   Over 3,000 now arrested in strike

● **6 June**   10,000 pickets at Orgreave: 93 arrests; 73 police and hundreds of pickets injured. Thatcher's involvement in avoiding rail strike revealed by Daily Mirror

● **8 June**   NUM and NCB meet for talks. Miners' march and lobby of Parliament in London – 120 arrested

● **13 June**	Talks break down
● **15 June**	NUM picket Joe Green killed by a lorry whilst picketing Ferrybridge power station
● **18 June**	Battle of Orgreave of nearly 10,000 pickets and 4,000 police. 93 arrests and 59 injured including Arthur Scargill
● **27 June**	Railway workers hold 24-hour strikes in London to support NUM. ISTC leaders say they will accept coal from anywhere
● **2 July**	Notts area council elections – strikebreakers take control
● **5-6 July**	NCB and NUM meet for talks
● **9 July**	National docks strike called over British Steel's use of scab labour at Immingham to unload iron ore
● **10 July**	Court order granted to Notts miners forbidding NUM conference from passing rule change allowing disciplining of working miners
● **10-11 July**	NUM conference passes disciplinary rule changes
● **13 July**	Arrests made in strike pass 4,000 mark
	Government withholds tax refunds to striking miners
● **18 July**	High Court grants Notts NUM application to have rule changes made null and void
	Talks collapse over issue of uneconomic pits
● **19 July**	Thatcher makes her speech to Tory backbench committee calling the miners the "enemy within."
● **22 July**	First national conference of Women Against Pit Closures
● **23 July**	Dockers call off strike
● **28 July**	NUM and TUC hold talks
● **31 July**	South Wales NUM fined £50,000 for contempt of court, refuse to pay and assets seized
● **1 August**	Mass demonstration outside South Wales NUM in Pontypridd against threat of sequestration. Labour Party Young Socialists (LPYS) mobilise hundreds to attend from their summer camp in the Forest of Dean
● **6 August**	Two Yorkshire miners apply to High Court for ballot in Yorkshire
● **10 August**	Special NUM conference reaffirms disciplinary rule changes and calls on TUC for support
● **11 August**	20,000 march in Women Against Pit Closures demonstration in London
● **13 August**	Police refuse to co-operate with National Council for Civil Liberties regarding the policing of the strike
● **15 August**	South Wales miners occupy sequestrators Price Waterhouse's offices in Birmingham
● **16 August**	Sequestrators claim to have seized £707,000 direct from South Wales NUM accounts

- **20-24 August** Police battle with pickets for five days to get one scab into Easington colliery, Durham
- **30 August** South Wales miners seize transporter bridge in Newport and 110 miners occupy BSC jetty at Port Talbot for 56 hours – Militant supporters amongst them
- **September** (a month of battles at pit heads as NCB attempt to stir up back-to-work movement)
- **3 September** 5,000 organised through Broad Left Organising Committee (BLOC) lobby the TUC, which votes to support NUM
- **9 September** Talks resume
- **15 September** Talks break down again
- **19 September** Second docks strike ends
- **28 September** NACODS votes by 82.5% in favour of strike
High Court rulings declare North Derbyshire and Yorkshire strikes illegal
- **30 September** Neil Kinnock tries, unsuccessfully, to get motions criticising police actions during the miners' strike off the Labour conference agenda
- **1 October** Arthur Scargill and four other NUM leaders served with writ on floor of Labour conference. Scargill gets standing ovation at the conference
- **2 October** Kinnock's speech to the conference "abhors all violence".
Over 7,000 have been arrested during the strike and 40 jailed
- **3 October** NACODS and NCB go to conciliation service ACAS
- **9 October** Tory Party conference sees Home Secretary Leon Brittan guarantee government money for policing strike
- **10 October** NUM fined £200,000 and Arthur Scargill fined £1,000 for contempt of court
- **11 October** New talks at ACAS
- **15 October** Talks fail – NCB insists on its right to manage and close 'uneconomic' pits
- **19 October** Power workers in EEPTU union, led by extreme right wingers, vote by 84% not to support miners
- **20 October** Michael Eaton, area director in North Yorkshire, appointed as NCB spokesperson instead of the incompetent MacGregor
- **24 October** NACODS call off strike after changes made to colliery review procedure by NCB to avert strike
- **25 October** High Court orders seizure of NUM funds after union refuses to pay contempt of court fine
- **28 October** Sunday Times story detailing NUM executive Roger Windsor's visit to Libya. Windsor later claimed to be MI5 spy in Seumas Milne's book The Enemy Within
- **29 October** NCB removes Eaton as spokesperson after only nine days, to be reinstated shortly afterwards

● **3 November**   Kinnock announces he is too busy to speak at major NUM rallies

High Court forbids North Derbyshire NUM from spending any more money on the strike

Price Waterhouse seizes NUM assets

Special delegate conference reaffirms strike continues

● **6 November**   3,000 attend mass NUM rally, Edinburgh

● **8 November**   6,000 at NUM rally in Sheffield

● **9 November**   Mass picket at Cortonwood to stop one miner attempting to scab

● **11 November**   NCB offers £650 Christmas bonus to striking miners returning to work before 19 November

● **12 November**   Thatcher compares pickets to IRA bombers

● **13 November**   TUC general secretary, Norman Willis, confronted by hangman's noose at miners' rally in South Wales, after he attacks "the brick, the bolt and the petrol bomb"

● **21 November**   Government announces further £1 to be deducted from state benefits paid to striking miners' families in addition to non-existent £15 strike pay already deducted

● **1 December**   Herbert Brewer appointed as receiver solely in charge of NUM funds

8,731 arrested, 87 gaoled and 17 sent to detention centres at this point in strike

● **3 December**   Brewer fails to claim NUM funds held in Luxembourg

● **7 December**   Brewer resigns, Michael Arnold takes over

TUC rules out 'illegal' action in support of the miners

● **14 December**   Energy minister, Peter Walker, rejects further talks

● **20 December**   Notts area council changes rules to 'loosen' ties with national NUM

1985

- **1 January**   Kent miners Terry French and Chris Tazey sentenced to five years and three years respectively as arrests climb to over 10,500 (9,145 in England and Wales; 1,406 in Scotland)
- **12 January**   Pro-strike Notts NUM leader Henry Richardson suspended from office by right-wing strikebreakers
- **17 January**   One-day rail strike in Yorkshire and East Midlands in support of railway workers sacked at Coalville depot
- **24 January**   NUM executive agrees to meet NCB following meeting between NCB director Ned Smith and NUM general secretary Peter Heathfield
- **29 January**   Preliminary talks break down
- **19 February**   TUC meets Thatcher and Walker and produces final document
- **20 February**   NUM rejects TUC document but accepts review procedure as agreed by NACODS and asks for talks with no preconditions
- **21 February**   Special delegate conference rejects TUC document
- **24 February**   Big London demonstration in support of miners leads to 101 arrests after police attack the march
- **28 February**   NCB announce that sacked miners will not be reinstated
- **1 March**   Durham, Lancashire, South Wales and COSA vote for return to work without agreement. Scottish executive agrees same but with rider that this is dependant on an amnesty for 700 sacked miners
- **2 March**   Yorkshire votes by four votes to continue strike
- **3 March**   NUM special delegate conference votes by 98-91 to return to work without an agreement or amnesty
- **4 March**   Scotland delegate conference votes 7-6 to stay out
Yorkshire votes to go back
Kent votes to stay out
- **5 March**   Miners in South Wales and Yorkshire return behind brass bands with their supporters.
Some South Wales and Yorkshire miners turn back at picket lines mounted by Kent miners
Half of Yorkshire miners still out, as are half Scottish miners and all Kent miners
Scottish miners' delegates vote 10-5 for return to work
- **6 March**   10,000 miners still striking in Yorkshire, Scotland and Kent
- **10-11 March**   Kent and Scotland last areas to vote to return to work
700 sacked miners still not reinstated into former jobs

South-East TUC Demonstration, London, 27 June 1985
photo by Mick Carroll

THE GREAT miners' strike of 1984-85 was the longest lasting, most bitter industrial dispute of the second half of the 20th century in Britain and was undoubtedly the most widespread in its effects on society generally.

It was one of the most momentous events ever in British labour movement history and had a huge impact on virtually every subsequent industrial and political development.

Over 27 million working days were lost in strike action in 1984 (mainly amongst miners). Two miners, David Jones and Joe Green, were killed while picketing. 11,300 miners and their supporters were arrested and over 5,600 stood trial and more than a hundred were jailed, although 1,504 were released without charge. Striking Nottinghamshire miners had curfews and a pass system imposed on them – like the hated apartheid system in South Africa – which meant they were virtually under house arrest on occasion.

Seafarers were sacked and railworkers were victimised for taking solidarity action with the miners. Over 700 miners were sacked and not reinstated in their jobs.

The state benefit system was abused to try and starve the miners back.

In response to all of this, over £60 million was raised for the miners, according to the Guardian newspaper. Warehouses full of food and toys were donated to the striking miners and their families from trade unionists and supporters in Britain and internationally.

A huge network – an alternative welfare state in effect - started and inspired by the miners themselves and the miners' wives support groups, mushroomed and spread across the five continents of the globe.

In particular the strike saw thousands of miners' wives come to the forefront; not solely organising background assistance but going on picket lines and travelling throughout Britain and the world explaining the miners' just cause.

Women played a vital role in the strike. Sue Alberry from Clowne, a North Derbyshire village with half a dozen local pits described how the local Women's Action Group started from scratch to build this support: *"Our group of miners' wives and other local women gave out 300-400 food parcels every week until the end of the strike. When we needed to feed pickets, there was no electricity or hot water in our strike centre, but we were given camping stoves, gas lamps, tables and forms and we were soon cooking 200-500 breakfasts a day. We started a two shift-system - one week picketing, one week in the centre. A local shopkeeper gave us buckets of hot water from his shop, another gave us bread rolls. The butcher wouldn't give us anything and his shop was boycotted for years afterwards.*

"In the school summer holiday we supplied hot meals for the kids. We found clothes, prams and cots for babies born during the strike. At Christmas we organised a party at

a local pub with a striking miner as Santa - all the kids got a small present. The hardest part was when they went back to work. We marched back with them, heads held high because we did what was right. I felt proud to have been part of this strike." [1]

This huge collective effort in backing the miners meant that Tory prime minister Margaret Thatcher did not get the short, sharp victory she hoped for against her old class enemy. And the events of the miners' strike have left a legacy of bitterness and class hatred that has remained for decades to haunt the Tories.

The Tories later admitted that it cost nearly £6 billion to win the dispute, which they saw as a political attempt to break the power of the National Union of Mineworkers (NUM). And from 1985-95 the Tories' continued war against the miners cost at least £28 billion spent in destroying the coal industry through redundancy and benefit payments, keeping pits mothballed and lost revenue from coal. According to Dave Feickert, the NUM national research officer from 1983-93: *"This is nearly half of the North Sea tax revenues of £60 billion collected since 1985."* [2]

It was estimated that over £10 billion was spent switching coal-fired power stations to dual coal and oil use before and during the strike.

Thatcher and her cabinet were desperate for victory and prepared to go to great lengths - the police were openly used as a political weapon. Former Tory chancellor Nigel Lawson admitted that preparation for the strike was *"just like rearming to face the threat of Hitler in the 1930s"*. For the first time in a post-war national strike the police were brought out before the public's gaze as an openly political arm of the state and an increased suspicion and lack of confidence in them has remained since. Agents provocateurs, spies and the army were also deployed.

MI5 and MI6 were involved. Shadowy right wingers like David Hart and Tim Bell, who were Thatcher's undercover advisers during the dispute, have since boasted about their connections with the intelligence communities and the funding they received from big business. And former trade union leaders like Joe Gormley of the NUM and other union officials, it is claimed, were working for MI5, including Roger Windsor, who was chief executive of the NUM during the strike.[3]

Yet, despite the extraordinary lengths the Tories went to, by October 1984, six months into the strike, the future of Thatcher's government hung in the balance - when there were less than six weeks' coal stocks left. The proposed strike by the pit supervisors' union NACODS threatened to close down all working pits in the Midlands at this time.

Former chairman of the Central Electricity Generating Board (CEGB), Sir Walter Marshall, spelt out what this meant: *"Our predictions showed on paper that Scargill would win certainly before Christmas. Margaret Thatcher got very worried about that... I felt she was wobbly".* [4]

lan MacGregor [5], the Thatcher-appointed boss of the National Coal Board (NCB), was summoned to Downing Street and recalls Thatcher's comments in his memoirs: *"I'm very worried about it. You have to realise that the fate of this government is in your hands Mr MacGregor. You have got to solve this problem".* [6]

The Iron Lady melts

BUT IT wasn't the determination of the 'Iron Lady' Thatcher or any other Tories that saved them - it was the trade union and Labour leaders. The union leaders claimed they couldn't deliver support for the miners but the experience at rank-and-file level was that workers were ready to come out in support.

A poll even in the dying days of the strike, when it was clearly heading to defeat, showed that 40% of trade unionists still supported the miners and 35% - many of whom would have been in key sections that could have determined the outcome of the strike - were willing to take action.

Even at that stage, with the correct call and leadership, such support could easily have been built into a force of two to three million workers. This force could have taken the generalised solidarity strike action that may have staved off the miners' bitter defeat and possibly even have brought victory.

Ned Smith, the former director of Labour relations at the NCB commented in a TV interview after the strike that the failure of the Trade Unions Congress (TUC) to deliver *"total support"* for the miners was the turning point in the attitude of the government. [7]

Some Left union leaders genuinely wanted to help but lacked the elementary tactics, strategy and confidence to do so. We commented at the time that unfortunately *"the infection of new realism [the class-collaborationist rightward drift of the union movement] had even spread to the Left leaders"*, who only gave the most general of calls for solidarity action with very little concrete being done in practice.

However, when the dockers came out in July, there was talk in Tory government circles of calling a *"state of emergency"*. And on a number of occasions, Thatcher personally intervened behind the scenes in pay negotiations, such as the railworkers and power workers, to increase their offer and ensure a second front didn't open. Car workers, after years of being under the cosh of Thatcherite bosses, began to recover their confidence and were also given a generous pay settlement when they threatened action.

Miners still defiant – 20 years on

AMONGST MANY miners and their families and supporters there is still a huge pride in their battle from 1984-85 struggling so magnificently when such odds were stacked against them. But it still sticks in their throats to be told their struggle was doomed from the start and that they were only being used as pawns in an ideological battle between Margaret Thatcher and Arthur Scargill.

They were not, as right-wing electricians' leader Eric Hammond insultingly described them: *"Lions led by donkeys."* The miners' strike was clearly not orchestrated by NUM leaders like Scargill, but started from below as a defensive struggle to stop the rundown of their industry and to preserve their communities.

Striking miner Dave Nixon summed up the mood of many young miners when he told a BBC documentary in 2004: *"In February 1984 we were like a coiled spring ready to be triggered... Of course we knew it would be a long strike but we were willing to suffer the two months we thought it would take to convince the Coal Board that their arguments were unjust."*

The reality was that the national and area NUM leaderships knew what was coming – particularly with the build up of coal stocks - but were not certain about how and in what way their struggle would develop. Certainly, much of the leadership appears to have been caught off guard at the beginning of the strike, which produced a cautiousness and hesitancy in the early days which led to complications later on.

Even leading figures on the Left who were solidly behind the strike pessimistically concluded early on that the miners would not win. In Tony Benn's diary entry for 5 May 1984 he wrote: *"It looks as though the miners cannot beat the government."* [8] He did, however, predict a long strike.

Yet, once the strike started it developed its own logic. It was clearly seen by the miners and their supporters in the wider working class, as well as by the Tories and the ruling class, as a battle that had to be fought to the finish. On a number of occasions during the dispute the government wavered when it saw partial strike action in support of the miners from other sections of workers.

The class struggle is not decided in advance like a mathematical formula. It can only be decided in the course of struggle itself and the miners understood that - even if they felt the odds were against them. It is better to fight and aim to win rather than go down to defeat without any resistance.

The support the miners' battle engendered showed that the working class was massively with them – even if most of the leadership of the workers' organisations were not.

Labour leader Neil Kinnock only visited a picket line once during the dispute nearly ten months into the strike. For most of the time before that he had hypocritically and equivocally claimed to support the miners whilst repeatedly condemning picket line 'violence'.

Whilst some former miners' leaders and the majority of the trade union and Labour leaders have moved far to the right since the strike – almost occupying a parallel universe - the miners who took strike action have not had regrets, nor repudiated their stand.

Joe Owens, a Scottish miner who was a Militant supporter during the strike, summed it up in a book he wrote marking the tenth anniversary of the strike: *"I feel privileged to have fought it. I wept when it ended and on the day three years later when they shoved us out on the stones with shitpence compensation; and I wept again in 1992 when another 30,000 men and their families faced what men I knew had faced. Everything to do with the experience is still raw and ten years later the rage is still with me. I think it always will be."* [9]

Other miners still feel the same 20 years on. One such is Brian Wilson of Brampton, near Cortonwood: *"I would go through it again... it was the notion of comradeship, of them against us, standing back to back... everybody were together. It were a thing I wouldn't have missed."* [10]

His wife, Anne Wilson showed what a revolution in consciousness the strike meant for the women who got involved: *"A lot of the women who supported the strike had never gone out to work; they just looked after the family and that were the way the miners wanted it to be. Then suddenly they came into their own. You see, the women found a voice, they found education and work – and that's something they never lost."* [11]

Yet, it was about much more than the 'spirit of 1984'. The miners' strike became an ideological battle about the future direction of society. Militant warned at the time that the Tories wanted to reduce mining and trade unionism to a *"mere memory"*. They have since virtually annihilated the coal industry and undermined manufacturing industry to a point where even sections of the ruling class can see that such a collapse is not in the long-term interests of British capitalism.

Mail on Sunday columnist Suzanne Moore put it succinctly enough: *"What their strike represented to us was a set of values worth fighting for. It was never simply about pay. It was about the threat Thatcher's free-market philosophy meant to their way of life, to their communities, to the very idea of trade unions."* [12]

Yet, the miners' struggle ensured that the imprint of militant trade unionism, though weakened, remained strong enough to survive the difficult period of the 1990s and is currently resurfacing.

It would take dozens of books to recall all the sacrifice and heroism of the miners' struggle and the detailed events of 1984-85. But as well as the fighting tradition of the miners we need to pass on to a new generation the lessons – political, strategical and tactical – from the 1984-85 miners' strike.

NOTES

1 From *The Socialist*, issue 337, 13 March 2004

2 *The Guardian*, 11 February 2004

3 For a full account of Windsor's role (along with that of Hart and Bell and MI5) see *The Enemy Within*, Seumas Milne, Verso, London 1994 and 2004

4 Interviewed on a Channel Four Dispatches programme in 1994

5 According to Paul Routledge, after Tory cabinet minister Lawson persuaded Thatcher to give Gormley a peerage he "maintained close links with the former electricians' union boss Frank Chapple, 'who detested Scargill and was at one with me in longing for a Coal Board management capable of standing up to him".

   "Chapple advised him to get someone who was not afraid of Scargill. Most businessmen said they weren't but in their hearts they were, he told Lawson after a dinner a deux. 'The Chapple test was one good reason why I went for MacGregor,' he wrote." (Paul Routledge, *Scargill the Unauthorised biography*, Harper Collins 1993, p132)

6 Quoted in *The Enemies Within*, Ian MacGregor with Rodney Tyler, Fontana 1985, p281

7 Quoted in Peter Taaffe, The Rise of Militant, Militant publications, London 1994

8 Quoted in Paul Routledge, *Scargill the Unathorised Biography*, p147

9 *Miners 1984-1994, A Decade of Endurance*, edited by Joe Owens, Polygon, Edinburgh 1994, p4

10 Brian Wilson quoted in *Observer Magazine*, 1 February 2004

11 Anne Wilson quoted in *Observer Magazine*, 1 February 2004

12 *Mail on Sunday*, 7 March 2004

Tower Colliery, South Wales, 14 January 1983
photo by Militant

chapter 2 **The gathering storms**

THE SEEDS of the 1984-85 miners' strike were planted years before the strike started in March. The defeats the miners inflicted on the Tory government in 1972 and 1974 represented a political earthquake that resulted in Ted Heath's removal from office in February 1974. Key strategists of the ruling class determined that never again would a strike or trade union action be allowed to determine the fate of 'their' government. In particular they decided that the power of the miners, along with other unions, needed to be smashed – even if this meant the destruction of whole sections of British manufacturing.

Coal Board boss Ian MacGregor had announced in the autumn of 1983 that he planned to close 20 pits and axe 25,000 jobs in the mining industry. But it was when the proposed closure of Cortonwood colliery in south Yorkshire was announced on 5 March, that a walk-out of Yorkshire miners was provoked which rapidly began to escalate. The NCB area director announced Cortonwood's immediate closure without going through the accepted pit closure review procedure, in order to meet MacGregor and Thatcher's imposed cut in production levels. This was seen by the rank-and-file miners as the gauntlet being thrown down.

A few other pits in Yorkshire had already walked out. Within days most of the coalfield was strike bound and the area became the militant hub of the strike, sending out flying pickets to other areas.

Since the Tories' election in 1979, 47,000 mining jobs had been lost and 48 pits had been closed. Even after Arthur Scargill's election as NUM president in late 1981 over 20,000 mining jobs were lost and 21 pits closed.

However, during this time all pit closures were subject to the review procedure. This involved all mining unions being involved before accepting closure on the grounds of exhaustion or safety: alternative jobs were then provided for those miners wishing to remain in the industry. Mining is an extractive industry and inevitably some mines will close through natural exhaustion of mineable coal.

But the threat to Cortonwood was of an altogether different character from all other pit closure proposals. The shady hands of MacGregor and Thatcher were behind this attempt at a more rapid downsizing of the industry.

The decades of decline

AFTER THE coal industry's nationalisation in 1947, there followed decades of a slow, haphazard decline in the size of the industry and the number of men (and a few women) employed in and around the pits. In 1948 over 600,000 worked in the industry, by 1984 this was just 182,000.

On average, between eight to ten pits closed every year in this period and more pits closed under Labour governments than Tory ones. However, Thatcher's Tory government was going for a much bigger cull.

In the post-second world war years, certain elements of workers' control over issues like health and safety and hiring and firing had developed in the nationalised industry, particularly at local level through the efforts of the NUM. At a national level, however, despite having Communist Party (CP) members as NUM general secretary like Arthur Horner (1945-59) and Will Paynter (1959-68), the NUM's reputation for militancy was based on past struggles.

This period of CP rule saw no official strike action taken by the union against gradual pit closures and a correspondingly serious decline in miners' living standards until the 1970s. The NUM, which was formed from the Miners' Federation of Great Britain (MFGB) in 1944, had never organised national strike action on any issue until the 1972 strike over pay.

The state of labour relations in the coal industry at the time is revealed by a statement by Lord Robens, NCB chairman, on the decisive pro-management role of Will Paynter in the 1964 national wage negotiations: *"Paynter was still a Communist, which made his speech all the more remarkable, but his devotion to the union and the men whose well being was his responsibility, as always, came before his party's affiliations... He told his hearers he accepted the board's offer of nine shillings and sixpence per week [about 50p a week] on the minimum was the most the industry could afford... Paynter saved the day."* [1]

In 1948, miners' wages were 29% above the average pay of manual workers. By 1960 they were only 7.4% above and by 1970 they were 3.1% below the average. The introduction of the national power loading agreement (NPLA) in 1966 helped overcome some of the problems miners had faced in getting paid a proper national rate for the job by introducing a standard wage structure for the industry.

In previous bonus scheme deals (where workers were paid according to how much they produced without taking into account the hours worked or geological complexities at a pit). The NPLA made sure miners no longer faced the incessant battles over their rate and for once they knew how much they would be paid every week.

Resurgent tide of struggle

THERE HAD been a resurgence of the traditional miners' militancy below the surface in a number of key coalfields in the late 1960s. In Yorkshire, a traditionally right-wing area of the union, the creation of the Barnsley Miners' Forum in 1967 led to the development of a new generation of left-wing leaders emerging from the rank and file – foremost among them was Arthur Scargill.

The Barnsley Miners' Forum was to play a crucial role in organising successful unofficial industrial action on pay and conditions in the 1960s, which developed the methods of flying pickets and mass picketing used so successfully in 1972 and 1974.

The reputation of the miners as the militant brigade of guards of the labour movement was won through its heroic struggles at the start of the 20th century and their nine-month struggle and defeat in 1926.

The miners retied the knot of history as a militant class-struggle union in the 1970s – a period of heightened industrial and political action – where they were at the forefront of workers' struggles, organising solidarity and inflicting the humiliating defeat of Heath.

The rising curve of industrial militancy in the early 1970s is shown through the number of days lost of all workers in strike action:

1970	10,908,000 days lost
1971	13,589,000 days lost
1972	23,923,000 days lost

The figure for 1972 has only been surpassed three times in the recorded history of strike action in Britain: in 1926 the year of the general strike, in 1979 through the so-called winter of discontent strike by public-sector workers against the Labour government's pay freeze and in 1984 itself (27 million days) because of the miners' strike.

From 1969-70 onwards a series of industrial demonstrations and strike movements against the industrial relations policies – an attempt to restrain the growing influence and power of trade unions amongst the working class – of first the Wilson Labour government of 1964-70 and then the Heath Tory government of 1970-74 had greatly radicalised and politicised huge swathes of trade union activists and workers generally.

Mass demonstrations, strike movements and even a threatened one-day general strike took place against the Heath government's anti-union legislation. In particular, action against the jailings of the Pentonville Five London dockers and the Shrewsbury Two building workers in 1974 under the Industrial Relations Act and the occupation of Upper Clyde Shipbuilders, showed the heightened consciousness and militancy of workers at that time.

Into this arena stepped newly confident and militant miners in 1972 winning a huge victory for higher wages, which helped erase the bitter memories of the defeat of 1926. The miners gained victory because the NCB and the government were unprepared for the strike, reckoning that a right-wing national leadership could avert the threat of action and that the post-war consensus about managing the industry would continue.

The flying pickets

ANOTHER KEY factor in the strike was the more widespread development of flying pickets and mass picketing. A pivotal point was the closure of the gates at Saltley coke depot – a coal storage depot for the foundries and industry in the Midlands. On 10 February 1972, 10,000 miners, engineering and car workers descended on Saltley Gates – as well as strike action being taken that day by over 100,000 workers in the area after Arthur Scargill, president of the Yorkshire miners at the time, addressed mass union meetings. This then forced the police officer in charge to demand the closure of the gates.

Miltant, the forerunner of the Socialist Party, played a significant part in this action: *"Militant supporters in Birmingham had played a key role in tipping off the NUM pickets in Birmingham that Saltley Gate was being used as a collecting depot for 'scab coal'."* [2]

Then the miners' action really began to bite and successfully ended decades of divisions over pay between pits and areas.

These tactics were again put to use in the industrial action of 1974, following an overtime ban from the end of 1973, although on a lesser scale than in 1972. The Heath government, still licking its wounds from 1972, was more consciously trying to take on the miners and break them this time round.

However, Heath had still not prepared in the same way as Thatcher was to prepare a decade later. The miners had instituted an overtime ban before strike action, which was coupled with electrical power workers refusing to work around the clock. This alone was enough to bring in a *"state of emergency"*, with petrol rationing, power cuts and the infamous three-day working week.

The Times newspaper, then seen as a more authoritative voice for the interests of British capitalism said: *"We cannot afford the cost of surrender"*, outlining an intent for a fight to the finish with the organised working class.

The Times also raised the shadowy threat of more dictatorial measures to beat the miners' action saying that *"the only remaining choice is to impose a policy of sound money at the point of a bayonet."* [3] The moves towards an authoritatarian solution were constantly being explored behind the scenes during this period. [4]

With an effective two-day-a week lock out declared on the working class, Prime Minister Heath then called an election in February 1974 where he asked 'Who rules the country?' The answer he got was that it was not him or his Tory Party. In one of the most polarised ever general elections – with the miners' strike ongoing – Heath was turfed out of office. The success of flying pickets and mass picketing was to form a key part of the psychology and preparations of militant miners in the run-up to and during the 1984-85 strike.

But the ruling class learnt lessons from the strikes of 1972 and 1974 and made preparations accordingly for the brutal class war they conducted in 1984-85. The NUM leaders were aware of the preparations made by the Tory government elected in 1979 (through the Ridley Report and other measures, of which more later, that represented a qualitative change in the thinking of sections of the ruling class). But they were still reliant on the tactics of 1972 and 1974 to win their next strike.

It was not that the tactic of flying pickets and mass picketing were wrong or inappropriate. However, because of a number of fundamental differences they could not be the sole means of winning victory in an all-out bitter political dispute that 1984-85 was to become.

One factor working against a cohesive national struggle on either pay or pit closures was the effective imposition of divisive bonus payments in 1978, despite a national ballot voting against it by 55%. The Left successfully argued against reintroducing the scheme, which was hated in many areas, because it set miner against miner and pit against pit. The right-wing areas and national leadership, including NUM President Joe Gormley defied a national conference decision against the scheme and tried to subvert it by gaining a High Court ruling to hold a ballot.

When the ballot went against them they declared it null and void. Then the Left challenged this constitutional fraud at the High Court where Mr Justice Watkins said: *"The result of a ballot nationally conducted is not binding upon the National Executive Committee."*

Incredibly, this was a ruling the right wing chose to forget in 1984.

And it opened the floodgates for the incentive schemes. This meant once again that a miner in one pit could earn only £6 a week in bonus payments whereas a miner in an allegedly more productive pit nearby could earn over £40 a week. The variations between areas were further enhanced by the differential bonus payments. Such divisions were to be a factor in later national pay ballots and indeed in the 1984 strike.

The Tories regroup and prepare for showdown

EVEN BEFORE its election in 1979, the Tory Party, egged on by the ruling class who wanted to curb the effective power of the unions, made industrial and political preparations to take on the miners. Their reasons were many fold, with revenge not the least amongst their motives. But, as has been subsequently shown, the Tories were using their war against the miners to attempt to weaken and break the power of organised labour. They were willing to carry through a deindustrialisation of key sectors of Britain where working-class opposition to the Tories had been strongest.

Coupled with this was the attempt to smash local democracy in councils like Liverpool and Lambeth, which opposed – successfully for a period – the Thatcher government's plans. These meant the impoverishment and destruction of parts of inner-city Britain through a massive programme of cuts in public spending as part of their monetarist programme.

The key elements in the Tories' preparations for the events of 1984-85 were the implementation of the Ridley Report proposals, which was 'leaked' in the Economist in 1978. This infamous report was written by Nicholas Ridley who was later to become a Tory cabinet minister and Lord. It proposed the following:

- A building up of coal stocks to see power supply last throughout a lengthy miners' strike.
- The increasing use of private, non-union haulage companies to carry coal.
- Some power stations were switched to dual coal and oil burning.
- A massive tooling up and increase of police powers was to be combined with more draconian civil (anti-union) and criminal laws during the strike.

The Tories did all this and more with a vengeance. From 1980 to 1983 coal stocks were built up from 37.7 million tonnes to 58 million tonnes. And in 1981 the Central Electricity Generation Board was asked by Sir Donald Maitland, Permanent Secretary at the Department of Energy, to prepare a contingency plan to cope with a miners' strike. It was ready within a few months.

This followed on from the Thatcher government's humiliating climbdown at the hands of the miners in 1981, when South Wales miners' bold and determined action against pit closures began to spread throughout the British coalfields. The Iron Lady was forced to retreat without using any of her newly established legal powers, like the Employment Act.

The miners' victory in 1981, after the setback of the steel strike in 1980, gave confidence to other groups of workers taking industrial action but it was clear, as Militant warned at the time, that this was a temporary, tactical retreat. Thatcher and the ruling class would come back at a later stage, if they were allowed to, with further attacks.

Chronic underfunding

THE PITS, however, were also made to look increasingly uneconomic and liable to closure during this period by a process of starving the industry of funding. There was a continual rigging of the NCB accounts – to portray the industry as a loss-making operation - and an increasing use of the discovery of geological problems at pits by a new more hardline NCB management now headed by Ian MacGregor.[5]

The NCB was charged over £100 million in interest to store the millions of tonnes of coal that was stockpiled. Additionally, British coal had the lowest level of state subsidy in Western Europe.

West Germany	received £8.60 subsidy per tonne
France	received £17.20 subsidy per tonne
Belgium	received £17.70 subsidy per tonne
Britain	received £3.20 subsidy per tonne

Militant argued for the same level of subsidy to be applied to the British coal industry, as opposed to the argument put forward by the Communist Party and Labour Left that there should be controls limiting the import of coal from other countries. Import controls, Militant argued, would set miners in one country against another and would sow the illusion that there could be a 'national' solution to the looming crisis in Britain's coal industry at the expense of other miners abroad.

For a long time before the strike, and during it, Militant argued that whilst it was necessary to campaign against pit closures there also needed to be a socialist plan of production for the industry and a socialist, integrated energy policy. These demands were first featured in a Militant NUM programme for action produced as a pamphlet in late 1977.

It was clear then that at some stage there would be conflict over the future of the coal industry. The Plan For Coal drawn up by the NCB in 1973 had envisaged a much larger 'market' for coal than actually transpired in the early 1980s. In response to the threatened contraction of the industry we argued in the pamphlet for:

- Removal of the Coal Board's debt
- Open the books; no phoney accounting; scrap the interest charges
- End competition among nationalised industries
- No redundancies; fight all closures except on grounds of proven exhaustion or safety as determined by the union
- Work or full pay; alternative work at equivalent rates and benefits
- Combat the NCB propaganda on the need to stockpile coal
- For workers' control and management of the coal industry
- For the nationalisation of all private concerns in the fuel industry under workers' control and management
- For the setting up of a national fuel corporation
- For a socialist national fuel policy [6]

Thatcher insisted at the time that *"Marxists wanted to defy the law of the land in order to defy the laws of economics".* But in her memoirs she revealed: *"The coal strike was always about far more than uneconomic pits. it was a political strike."* [7]

During the strike Left-wing Oxford University economist, Andrew Glyn produced a pamphlet, commissioned by the NUM, which showed when many of the NCB's false overheads were stripped away the coal industry was not *"insolvent"* as the Tories claimed and *"the production of coal in 1983-84 more or less covered its underlying costs of production and financed the industry's investment."*

He also pointed out that when you added the devastating economic costs of shutting down pits then *"there is not one single pit whose closure would benefit government revenue".* He concluded that *"under present circumstances there is no economic case whatsoever for pit closure before exhaustion of mineable reserves."* [8]

The warning signs

HOWEVER, ALL of the Tory preparations for a showdown with the miners would have come to nothing if the Thatcher government had not been prepared to play its political hand more astutely than the leadership of the Labour Party or the TUC.

Thatcher and her ruling clique had gained confidence in the run-up to the 1984 strike following their 'success' in the Falklands/Malvinas conflict and winning the 1983 election against a Labour opposition weakened by the split and temporary rise of the Social Democrat Party – a right-wing breakaway from the Labour Party.

However, this combination of 'successes' would have not been enough, in themselves, to have given Thatcher the necessary confidence to take on the miners; especially given that Arthur Scargill had been resoundingly elected president in 1981 with over 70% of the vote.

Before Thatcher took on the miners a number of other key factors were to slot into place.

After the 1983 election defeat, Labour and trade union leaders, including the newly elected Labour Party leader, Neil Kinnock, advocated a policy of 'new realism'. This was a code for retreating in the face of the class enemy without firing a shot in retaliation. Politically this was the beginning of a long rightward march which has led to Blairism, the complete transformation of Labour into an openly pro-capitalist party.

The philosophical 'justification' for new realism was that the defeat of Labour in the 1983 election, with one of the most radical manifestoes in its history (falsely dubbed the longest ever suicide note in history by right-wing Labour MP Gerald Kaufman). This implied that socialist ideas were no longer popular and that accommodation with the bosses and the Tories had to be sought by the trade unions. Politically, arguments like those of CP academic and author Eric

Hobsbawn, arguing that the class composition of society was changing, the manual working class was dwindling and consequently the old class notions of solidarity etc were no longer applicable, were echoed by Neil Kinnock and his entourage.

Roy Hattersley, who now bemoans the rise and effects of Blairism, was an early advocate of 'new realism' and breaking the union link. In January 1984 when deputy leader of the Labour Party he told a Fabian Society lecture that *"trade unions are a diminishing force in British political and industrial life... the dependency of the party on them is something on which I do not believe we can rely in the future as we could in the past."* [9]

How wrong the ideas and practice of 'new realism' were would soon be shown by the Warrington NGA printworkers' struggle against Stockport Messenger Group owner Eddie Shah's attacks on the union in December 1983. Despite determined action by the printworkers and their supporters the Warrington dispute's ultimate defeat was to eventually prove the green light for the Tories to attack the miners.

It was the official policy of the TUC at the time to defy the anti-union laws and to defend any union that was threatened by them. This had been passed at a special conference in Wembley 1981.

From the weakness displayed by the TUC leaders during the Warrington battle, the Tories concluded that the union leaders would not be able to deliver solidarity action if the capitalist class launched a bitter and brutal offensive against the miners.

The Warrington dispute was the first time that the Tories' new anti-union laws were tested against the trade union movement. The NGA faced sequestration (seizure of its assets) after defying a court judgment of a £50,000 fine against the union. The nightly mass picketing at the Warrington plant saw the first appearance of the new beefed-up police forces under the Tories. Workers who had come from all parts of the country to support the printers were consistently and brutally attacked by the police.

Militant said at the time: *"The gloves are off. The ruling classes are out to destroy the print union the NGA... The Tories have declared war."*

The paper also demanded that the TUC should deliver on its commitment to general strike action. Despite it being the policy of the TUC, the call never came, apart from through Arthur Scargill.

The recently elected president of the NUM called for a 24-hour general strike at a meeting of 500 miners, rail and steel workers in Birmingham and argued that the TUC and Labour Party should show the same dedication and commitment to the NGA and our class as the Tories show to their class *"including the organisation of the most massive picket ever seen."* [10]

The strike could have been a famous victory, if the determination of rank-and-file workers who participated on the picket lines and supported the NGA had been matched by the union leaders on the TUC general council.

We called for an all-out printers' strike when the union was fined £650,000 and faced writs for damages of over £3 million from newspaper owners. Print bosses, like the notorious Robert Maxwell secretly approached Stockport Messenger Group owner Shah at one stage to settle, because of the fear of where the workers' struggles were leading.

Maxwell is alleged to have said: *"God help us all"* at the looming possibility of an all-out strike; an indication that the balance of class forces was still in the workers' favour at that stage.

But the right-wing TUC leaders abjectly gave in to the Tories' anti-union laws, urging the NGA and other print unions to stay within the law, and in so doing seriously undermined the power of the organised working class to resist the bosses' attacks.

However, the Left in the unions also had to take on board the lessons and some responsibility for the eventual debacle at Warrington. Militant argued at the time: *"The TUC general council, with its inbuilt right-wing majority, does not reflect the true balance of industrial power within the movement. The Left leaders of the TUC, therefore, those who supported the NGA must now be prepared to organise outside the framework of the TUC."* [11]

Shortly afterwards in an act of outright provocation, civil service trade union membership was banned at the government monitoring/spying centre GCHQ in Cheltenham; ostensibly on the grounds that their union membership threatened national security.

Again the union leaders meekly accepted the emasculation of union rights at GCHQ. They organised some token demonstrations and a day of protest involving over one million workers, but it was primarily an exercise in letting off steam.

And then the majority of the union leaders scurried away from the prospect of class war and buried themselves deep in their daily routines and the illusory hideaway of new realism.

Thatcher and the Tories were, however, just getting into their stride in practising their exceptionally brutal version of class war and were preparing to take on the miners in a once and for all showdown.

But, given the glaring weaknesses at the tops of the union movement, how ready were the miners and their leaders for what turned out to be the longest and most bitter industrial dispute in British union history?

NOTES

1 From the *Communist Party of Great Britain since 1920*, p153, by James Eadie and David Renton. Palgrave publishers, 2002

2 *The Rise of Militant*, Peter Taaffe, Militant Publications, London 1994, p57

3 This editorial essentially was arguing for the economic policy of monetarism – the linking of money supply to the country's Gross Domestic Product –, which the Thatcher government was to bring in with a vengeance in 1980-81.

4 Lord Mountbatten and former *Daily Mirror* owner Cecil King for instance were discussing the possibility of a coup against Wilson's Labour government.

5 Ian MacGregor was the asset-stripper who had recently downsized the steel industry, butchering capacity, closing steelworks and sacking tens of thousands of steel workers. He had also been deputy chairman at British Leyland and was instrumental in the sacking of Derek Robinson – Red Robbo – the CP union rep who had been leading the fight back against the Edwardes plan to downsize the company.

6 *Militant* issue 701 also carried a centre-page article outlining socialist plan for the coal industry

7 Quoted by Larry Elliot, *The Guardian*, 2 March 2004

8 *The Economic Case Against Pit Closures*, NUM, Sheffield 1984

9 *Militant*, issue 682, 13 January 1984

10 *Militant* issue 679, 12 December 1983

11 *Militant* issue 680, 16 December 1983

YOUR CLASS NEEDS
YOU

ALL STRIKES start hesitantly. For trade unionists and all working-class people, contrary to the popular tabloid myth, being on strike is not a normal way of life. It involves a huge shake up to the daily routine, the uncertainty of being without income and possibly losing your job as a result of the action. For all workers, taking striking action is always a last resort, rather than being seen as inevitable.

While the best union activists always hope for the best and prepare for the worst, even they would be the first to admit that they never fully prepare for strike action.

The innovativion and determination often associated on a broad scale with large sections of workers on strike tends to come as the strike gains momentum rather than at the beginning.

The miners at that time were one of the most experienced and organised groups of workers when it came to threatening or taking industrial action to defend their interests. They were meticulous in their preparation both in terms of political propaganda and many practical aspects of their action. Inevitably, however, there is always a certain rustiness, even amongst the most experienced union activists when strike action starts.

The 1984-85 miners' strike, however, started more chaotically than many would have expected – especially given the clear signals that had been emanating from the Tory government and the new regime of NCB boss Ian MacGregor.

Left win control of NUM

THE START of the 1984-85 strike should have found the miners in a relatively strong position. For the first time in many decades the union had a left-wing president, vice-president and left-wing general secretary.

Peter Heathfield, from North Derbyshire, had been elected general secretary only a few months before the strike, to replace the retiring Lawrence Daly. Although securing only a narrow victory over right-wing area official John Walsh, Heathfield had explicitly campaigned against the threatened job losses in the industry and in support of the overtime ban, supported by over 75% of miners.

But Militant warned at the time *"escalation of the dispute, to be effective must be before spring."*[1] This was in response to those on the Left who argued that the overtime ban could go on beyond the summer, already tensions were building up in some of the coalfields.

Communist Party member Mick McGahey had been the vice-president of the union from 1973. Also, the Left had an outright majority of 13-11 on the union's national executive.

However, that Left leadership had suffered a number of defeats (particularly in three ballots for industrial action on pay and pit closures since Arthur Scargill became president) in the run-up to the start of the strike in March 1984.

Generally, Left areas such as South Wales, Scotland, Kent and Yorkshire recorded majorities for industrial action for better wages, against pit closures and against the introduction of the incentive bonus scheme; forced through undemocratically by previous president Joe Gormley and the right wing.

Whilst there had been big votes against action in the areas like Notts and the Midlands that had generally benefited most from the bonus scheme – enough to tip the balance against national action - the votes against action had decreased at each ballot.

Peter Heathfield, though, only a few weeks before the strike told a joint LPYS/North Derbyshire NUM meeting that he doubted whether the younger generation of miners, who had big mortgages and took foreign holidays, would go on strike.

But it was the determined resistance of the younger miners especially, as the strike started, that developed the strike's momentum. This time there was no escape route for a younger generation: moving on to another pit when yours closed was becoming more difficult as was the possibility of finding jobs outside the mining industry.

And the miners' action especially struck a chord amongst younger people: *"At Port Talbot steelworks nearly 200 young people from local schools and tech colleges joined a mass picket [early on in the strike]. The headmaster ordered the pupils back to school but as one told the police who tried to bully them 'I'm furthering my education – I'm learning to be a picket because it's the only job I'll get round here."* [2]

Former Tory cabinet minister Norman Tebbit revealed in 1992, how worried the Tories were by the threats of miners' strike action in 1982 and 1983. He said that the 1984 strike had been a *"close run thing"* and 18 months earlier the miners would have almost certainly triumphed. [3]

It is an unfortunate irony of history that until March 1993 there had never been a successful NUM ballot for industrial action against pit closures. All successful ballots had been on pay. One reason for this lay in the NUM's structure, which gave enormous power to area union officials. On issues like pay there was a general national agreement, but pit closures affected some areas more than others.

In 1983 the South Wales area took strike action over the threatened closure of Tymawr/Lewis Merthyr, which had been endorsed by the national executive under Rule 41. South Wales miners then went to other areas such as Yorkshire but found them hesitant about taking action. When a national ballot was called, pits in other areas which had started to come out returned to work while voting took place.

They were then subjected to the most fierce capitalist propaganda and this resulted in a 61% vote against action. This caused some confusion and bitterness among South Wales miners at the start of the 1984-85 strike.

This was taken as another green light by the Tories for them to look at a larger scale pit closure programme and take on the militancy and power of the miners.

Weakness of the NUM Left

THE OLD Left leadership of the union in many areas, and even the new Left in areas like Yorkshire, had to a degree been partially infected by the virus of new realism and were beginning to lack confidence in the ability of workers – even the miners – to prosecute a successful struggle.

Just weeks before the strike, for example, the Left leadership in Scotland, dominated by the CP and its fellow travellers, had given mixed signals on pit closures by postponing action for three weeks over the threat to close Polmaise colliery, near Stirling. The CP-dominated Scottish NUM executive eventually told local NUM officials to go it alone in their efforts to save the pit.

Polmaise, like other pits, could have been an issue that sparked a national strike. Certainly all the combustible material was there - the surrounding areas had 25%-40% youth unemployment rates and there was an angry mood, which was dissipated by the CP-led Scottish area NUM.

Fallin Labour Party Young Socialists (LPYS), for example – led by local Militant supporters – organised a public meeting on the issue. With over 70 attending, local NUM officials said that a geological fault at the pit could be easily cleared within five weeks, opening up a coalfields, which could guarantee work at the pit for 30 years.

At the meeting a young miner said that in the previous three years he had been at four pits and at each one he had initially been promised 20 years' work but each one had subsequently shut down very soon.

But at Polmaise the area leadership acted as a brake on the young miners, and unfortunately perhaps there wasn't a local leadership prepared to push their area executive into taking action. By contrast, in Cortonwood a few weeks later the miners came out by themselves and forced the area executive to endorse their strike. Yorkshire miners then moved to picket other coalfields.

The federal structure of the NUM meant that each area had a high degree of autonomy and there was a long tradition of areas organising local action against pit closures, and then successfully picketing out others as South Wales had done in 1981.

However, whatever the mood of the rank-and-file miners, the area and national leaderships were still smarting from the previous ballot upsets.

Kent miners march through London, 7 April 1984
photo by Paul Traynor

Notwithstanding the courage and determination that was shown throughout the strike and after by the NUM national leaders, Arthur Scargill and Peter Heathfield, the beginning of the strike saw them caught off guard. Many NUM leaders had the perspective of the overtime ban, which had been solidly endorsed in a national ballot, continuing until the autumn of 1984 and then taking strike action.

Although ballots for industrial action against pit closures and on pay had been defeated, there had been an increasing vote for action on pay in all areas on the last ballot before the strike. Taking all these factors into consideration the Tories, through their henchman MacGregor, probably thought that the time was right for a pre-emptive strike in March 1984.

Lack of confidence

THE BALLOT defeats and lack of action in the previous year definitely caused some Left NUM leaders to lack confidence about strike action developing, even as the majority of Yorkshire miners – the biggest and strongest area of the union – came out.

The South Wales NUM leadership, for example, was traditionally one of the most militant. When its leadership recommended strike action in support of Yorkshire, it found that a majority voted against them at report back meetings at Lodges (local branches).

Only the decisive actions of miners like Tyrone O'Sullivan and South Wales NUM executive member Ian Isaac, turned around a situation where miners had initially voted not to come out in support of Yorkshire miners.

Ian Isaac, then Lodge Secretary of St John's NUM and a member of the South Wales NUM executive from 1983-87, has summed up (in an unpublished memoir) the unpreparedness of some of the left NUM leaders in the area. Ian notes that when the closure of Cortonwood colliery was announced, which sparked the 1984-85 strike, there *"was a hesitancy on the part of South Wales miners to be seen yet again as the ones to come out first. They also remembered the lukewarm reception they had the previous year when attempting to convince Yorkshire and other traditionally militant areas to join them on strike against pit closures."*

South Wales turns around

BECAUSE OF this confusion and caution the strike got off to an unsteady start. Although Kent came out more or less straight away, in Scotland and South Wales it took more persuasion to convince miners that this was the big one. In South Wales it took four days from Friday 9 March to Monday 12 March to clarify the strike decisively in action.

On 9 March the South Wales NUM executive recommended at a special conference in Hopkinstown that the South Wales lodges should support the strike action
that had started in Yorkshire and Scotland – only five out of 45 lodges voted against.

Amongst the general public of South Wales at that time there was a general
recognition that a battle against closures was inevitable and everyone rallied
behind the miners. For instance, sales of the Militant rocketed upwards after the
first few days of the Yorkshire miners being out and in anticipation of a national
strike.[4]

But, the traditional loyalty of South Wales miners to their leadership may have
been taken for granted by some of the area's leaders and a more uncertain, uneasy
mood had crept in amongst some of the miners, the older generation in particular.

At St John's pit in Maesteg, there was a mixed and polarised mood at the first
report back from the area conference. There was a two to one vote against strike
action at a meeting on 10 March.

The younger miners – who had most to lose through mass redundancies - were
furious and the whole of the Lodge Committee threatened resignation, although
the Lodge committee leaders (three of whom were Militant supporters) convinced
them not to resign but to stand firm.

Many of the older men had been initially lured by the enhanced redundancy
packages of over £30,000 for some that the government, through the agency of the
NCB, dangled in front of their noses.

This vote against the area and local leadership was repeated in a majority of pits
– militant and non-militant alike – throughout the coalfield, with only a handful of
exceptions. Undoubtedly this hesitation reflected a certain bitterness or lack of
trust that existed after the retreat on Lewis Merthyr in 1983. But it also reflected that
the ground had not been fully prepared amongst the miners by the traditionally
Left leadership.

A recall area conference the next day (Sunday 11 March) again confirmed that
South Wales would support the action but this time 17 lodges out of 45 voted
against. A vote at a Scottish NUM conference on the same day saw a 50-50 split on
whether or not to continue their action. Kent was 100% out by this time as was
Yorkshire but the picture was still mixed in other parts of the British coalfield.

The Old Left area leadership in South Wales were jittery and did not have
confidence about what would happen the following morning. In the end they left it
in the hands of younger militants like Ian Isaac and Tyrone O'Sullivan. They held
their nerve and organised pickets at all pits on the following morning to uphold the
decision of the area conference. Even then there was fighting on some picket lines
but by the end of that day most of South Wales came out and swelled the ranks of

striking miners to over 100,000.

After that, Ian Isaac remembers attending a meeting of the South Wales Area Executive where he and another left-winger argued, in the light of all pits and surface lodges now respecting picket lines after a shaky start, that *"we should hold further mass meetings to vote on supporting those on strike and consolidate the mandate expressed by miners not crossing picket lines.*

"This was argued against by a number of executive members including the president, Emlyn Williams, general secretary George Rees and vice-president Terry Thomas. They argued that it was too risky and what would happen if they voted against again? This was the expression of the kind of confidence that some leaders had in their members and this type of thinking would surface again over the arguments about a national ballot."

However, the executive then agreed that Lodges could reconvene mass meetings to vote again on supporting the strike action of the Yorkshire miners.

In St John's a recall Lodge meeting on 14 March reversed the previous vote with all but 30 of the 600 miners voting for all-out strike action against the pit closures after the miners had seen that Yorkshire was solid.

On Saturday 10 March there was a two to one vote against action at Blaengarw pit in the Garw Valley. Within days this had been transformed into a 300-80 vote in favour.

The national NUM leaders showed more determination and courage as the strike gained momentum but were clearly uncertain of the balance of forces at the start.

There was no doubt in anybody's mind that this was going to be a more protracted and difficult struggle than the strikes of 1972 and 1974. But a leadership, as well as taking account of the true balance of forces in any situation, also has to give a lead when the battle lines are drawn.

Tyrone O'Sullivan, then secretary of Tower Lodge NUM in South Wales (who was later to become chairman of the Tower Colliery workers' co-operative) told Militant early in the strike: *"It's not going to be easy but we can win".*[5]

Within a week over 80% of the miners were out on strike and 134 pits were strike-bound. But in Nottingham, the South Midlands and even the traditionally militant Northumberland area a majority of miners were still at work. This was to change over the coming days in Northumberland and Midlands but not in Nottingham.

In the Midlands and Staffordshire it was Militant supporters and other rank-and-file miners that worked to pull their pits out. Militant supporters played a crucial role at Littleton and Lea Hall pits. Combined with the efforts of pickets from other areas they managed to close 90% of the Midlands coalfield.

Undoubtedly, the forces that were to be ranged against the miners, which were

Labour Party Young Socialists marching in Pontypridd
photo by John Woulfe

apparent at least in outline before the strike started, were considerable. But such was the resistance of the miners, even despite its hesitant, chaotic start, that by the summer it was a strike that could have been won.

Within weeks a huge display of solidarity with mass meetings, rallies, concerts and fundraising for the miners had shot up. Particularly important to this was the establishment of the miners' support groups and the women's support groups.

However, even here the lack of a co-ordinated approach by the area and national leadership often led to a shambles about which groups of miners should be collecting in which areas; in particular the CP-influenced leaderships of areas were to play a negative role in this: a role which they were to extend during the strike to vendettas against other Lefts and any group of miners who threatened their 'leadership'.

The hesitations at the start of the strike were a complicating factor in most areas of the country, even the traditionally militant ones. Although generally overcome, these were a big contributory part of the running sore that the issue of a national ballot and the situation in the Nottinghamshire coalfield became.

NOTES

1 *Militant* issue 685, 3 February 1984
2 *Militant,* issue 697
3 From *The Enemy Within,* Seumas Milne, Verso, London 1994, p16
4 For example in Maesteg 43 copies of *Militant* were sold in an hour. Similarly in other South Wales mining communities the following sales were noted: Resolven 44; Blackwood 35 and Newbridge 113 (the last two were in Neil Kinnock's constituency)
5 *Militant* issue 691, 16 March 1984

Thatcher pulling NCB Chairman, MacGregor's strings

SINCE THE start of the strike and for 20 years since, much agonised comment has been made on whether or not the strike would have been more successful if a national ballot had been called - either before the strike or within the first few months of strike action as the militant areas came out.

Right-wing critics, and some on the Left, argue that the NUM's fundamental error was not calling a ballot, which undermined the whole basis of the strike and allowed the majority of miners in Nottingham to continue working. The NUM had a long tradition of democracy and balloting but it wasn't always the case that ballots were held for industrial action. Particularly on the issue of pit closures, with some areas more affected than others, there was a tradition of spontaneous walk-outs and a genuine feeling that 'secure' areas like Nottingham shouldn't be allowed to vote down strike action in other areas like Wales, Scotland and Yorkshire.

Tony Benn said on a television programme in July 2002 that even if there had been a successful national ballot it would have been overturned in Nottingham. Although possibly a section of Nottinghamshire miners may have ignored the strike call and crossed the picket lines, past experience would have suggested a majority could have backed the national union.

In the 1972 and 1974 strikes the Notts area voted against strike action on pay but still fully came out as part of the national strike. Henry Richardson, a left-winger opposed to pit closures, had been elected area secretary in January 1983. In 1984 Notts did have a ballot and 27% voted for strike action, still a minority, but only 19% had voted for action in the last ballot in 1983.

Even if there had been scabbing (strike-breaking), the numbers concerned would have been far fewer and, crucially, far less effective in terms of coal production used to undermine the solidarity and morale of striking miners and their supporters, if there had been a national ballot.

In the Midlands area, which had a hesitant start, the efforts of Militant miners had closed down 90% of the coalfield and a majority of Midlands miners were out for the duration of the strike. One test of miners' opinion on the first weekend of the strike for ITV's Weekend World showed that 62% supported the strike, 33% were against and 5% were don't knows.[1]

During the strike Militant maintained a united stand with the miners and NUM and argued against the hypocrisy of the right wing in the unions over the ballot and the way they lined up with the Tories to try and undermine the strike.

But after the strike we pointed out that, because of the way the issue was used in the movement to cut across the miners' struggle, a ballot should have been called, especially after the rule change at a special conference on 19 April, which allowed a 50%+1 majority for strike action (instead of the previous 55%+1). A ballot then, six weeks into the strike, would have seen a clear national mandate for strike action.

Striking Scottish miner Joe Owens commented ten years later: *"Tactically, there should have been a ballot. It was a catastrophic mistake not to call one, particularly after the special conference... No one seriously doubts a majority would have voted to continue the strike, we were already dug in by that time. It would have won the Nottinghamshire miners over before a combination of time and resentment made that hope impossible. The impetus would have swung back to the NUM, its critics disarmed... By the end of April the question had become academic to the vast majority of miners on strike, who constituted the vast majority in the coalfield, yet it was an opportunity lost and it cost the union dearly."* [2]

A *Sunday Times* Insight book produced shortly after the strike recalls opinion polls at the time that showed things were moving in the NUM leadership's direction should they call a ballot. A 13 April Mori poll for the Sunday Times amongst all miners confirmed what earlier opinions polls had begun to show and it counted: *"68% for, 26% against and 6% uncommitted [assuming that the don't knows would have failed to vote]... that would have produced an almost unassailable 72% vote in favour. Even Nottingham, the most resolutely reluctant area, had by now apparently revised its view from outright opposition to a 42:43 dead heat in the area council."* [3]

Even given the fallibility of opinion polls, the NUM leadership giving a lead at this point could have produced a thumping majority for action which would have cut across the excuses of the right wing and Labour leader Kinnock. It could have cut off the Tory lifeline of coal supplies to the power stations from the Midlands, which was to prove crucial at a later stage of the strike. Despite this, the lack of a ballot in itself did not defeat the miners – although it was undoubtedly a complicating factor.

The main reason the miners lost was because key trade union leaders refused to organise effective solidarity action, where the lack of a ballot was used as a 'get-out' clause.

The right-wing leader of the electricians' union Eric Hammond said after the strike that he would have supported bringing out power industry workers if the miners had held a ballot. Yet, this was a smokescreen to cover his inaction and later betrayal of the miners. He would have still done everything to prevent such action developing as was to be the case later on *(see chapter 7).*

The Achilles heel of federalism

THE FEDERAL structure of the NUM had its strengths and weaknesses. It had allowed the development of militant areas, such as South Wales from the early 20th century. Even the areas themselves were effectively federal structures. The South Wales miners were originally known as the Fed (as was the national union)

South Celynen picket line, South Wales, November 1984
photo by Craig Stennett

and Yorkshire, although right wing for a long time, had eight area panels (later cut to four) where the Left developed and organised unofficial action.

This allowed localised area industrial action under Rule 41 where the union's national executive had the power to endorse strike action in an area. This was how the strike developed in 1984. Rule 41 had been used sometimes by the Left to undermine right-wing attempts nationally to block action as area strikes spread to other areas through flying pickets, and miners refusing to cross picket lines.

But, conversely, it also could act as a brake on area and national action on key issues as well if miners from other areas refused to back those striking miners or tensions and friction arose – as was evidenced over Tymawr/Lewis Merthyr in 1983.

Traditionally, the union right wing use the call for ballots to delay or halt effective action. However, used effectively and prepared for by the Left, a successful and healthy ballot could have greatly enhanced the legitimacy of strike action as it did in 1972 and 1974.

There was a strong tradition in the NUM of individual pithead ballots and it was a respected means of addressing policy issues and legitimising disputes in the industry. Scargill and the Left either were not confident about getting a majority in any ballot or they thought the numbers on strike were sufficient in themselves and may have thought the chaotic way the strike was developing was a safer option.

The majority of miners were on strike. Less than 20% were at work at this stage and even less than that crossing picket lines as miners were not being allowed to mount pickets anywhere near the Nottingham coalfield after the Notts area ballot on 14 March 1984.

But for socialists and the best trade union activists, having a ballot to call or endorse action was not and is not an absolute principle – despite the anti-union laws. There are times where the momentum of action means having a ballot will be a backward step in organising the action.

For instance, in the postal workers' action in 2003 it would have been irresponsible to argue for a national ballot – especially given it now takes weeks to organise and implement – when effective strike action was taking place and spreading.

Indeed, postal ballots in particular are used by the right wing and ruling classes generally to rely on an inert layer in the trade unions to vote against action. Such a layer are subjected to a barrage of drivel and reactionary TV and media propaganda while the counter-arguments would only come out in detail at union meetings, as the capitalist media would not allow union activists a fair crack of the whip in explaining their case.

Those who are most directly involved in the union branches, workplaces committees and on the picket lines are the ones who can counter such arguments and mobilise greater numbers behind industrial action.[4]

But, given that recent ballots had not returned such a majority for action, to put the strike on hold – as the right wing in the NUM argued - while a national ballot was organised would have been wrong. Indeed the momentum for the strike was developing, as MacGregor initially planned to cut coal production from 101.4 million tonnes to 97.4 million tonnes, which entailed the closure of 20 pits and the axing of 25,000 jobs. Within a week these plans had been upped to mean the closure of 35 pits.

Scotland and Yorkshire had by this time voted for an all-out strike. Votes in South Wales were turning round in solid support of the strike after the area director Philip Weekes announced that six of the remaining 23 collieries in South Wales were now subject to review for closure.[5]

Within a week, despite initial votes against coming out, all but three South Wales pits were out on strike – and these were soon to follow. All were signs that even a difficult, messy start could be successfully turned round.

In areas where ballots were organised – even without proper picketing taking place - there were positive signs that if a national ballot were to be held then it would return the required majority. In a Midlands ballot the result was still a vote against action, but there was 17% more in favour of action than in a ballot just a few months previously.

If this trend had been repeated evenly across the country then the result would have been a majority for national action.

Making the strike solid

ALTHOUGH A ballot was not the must urgent issue on the agenda at that stage – certainly not to sriking miners - it was increasingly clear that the Tories had deliberately provoked the strike and hoped to whip up confusion surrounding the strike by raising the call for a ballot in a media offensive.

Militant said at the time that the key issues were to make the strike solid amongst the miners and take the case to the wider working class. We argued amongst miners there was a need to link the issue of protecting jobs with a national pay claim, as pit closures did not affect all areas of the NUM equally across the country.

In the wider working class, we called for a clear lead from the NUM's national leaders to consolidate the strike action and build a genuine Triple Alliance with the railworkers and steelworkers, and other workers whose jobs would also be affected. Such action was needed to stop the movement of all coal stocks and supplies.

The Transport and General Workers' Union (TGWU) had called on its members from early on in the strike not to allow the delivery of coal stocks. But making such a call was one thing, delivering it effectively was another.

Despite the absence of a ballot, 134 pits were out in support of the action within a week. South Wales miners and those from other coalfields were getting a friendly response in Nottinghamshire amongst both miners who had come out on strike and those still working. Yet, Militant supporters realised that mass picketing of Notts pits would not be enough to bring them out. Indeed, on many occasions it was impossible for many miners to get to or participate on picket lines given the role of the police (*see chapter 4*).

Militant supporters argued at this time that there needed to be properly organised meetings to address non-striking miners in areas like Notts, as well as picketing. South Wales miners visited all Notts pits in 1983 over Lewis Merthyr and addressed canteen meetings before setting up pickets. Things generally happened the other way round in 1984 where pickets were set up first and then there were attempts to talk after.

We also argued that in these key areas there should be dispensation given to striking miners to go back down the pits – especially when police were not allowing even local miners to talk on the picket line to those going in to work – and discuss with those miners who had doubts to try and win them over.[6]

It is still likely that had there been a vote against action in Nottinghamshire, then the putative leaders of the scab Union of Democratic Miners (UDM – which emerged after the strike from the working miners' committee set up by Thatcher's 'advisers' David Hart and Tim Bell) would still have used this to argue for Notts opting out of strike action.

But a ballot at a pivotal stage in the strike – when the majority of miners were out on strike – could have seen 60%-70% or more in favour of action. It could have been used to convince a large section of Notts miners to come out and possibly prevented the development or effectiveness of groups like the working miners' committee initiated by shadowy individuals like David Hart, Tim Bell and the infamous Silver Birch, Chris Butcher.[7]

The special conference

IT LOOKED to many as if the NUM leaders were preparing the way for a national ballot. A special national NUM conference was held in Sheffield on 19 April 1984. As well as receiving reports on the action around the coalfields, the conference took a decision to lower the threshold for action in a national ballot from 55% to 50%. Although a narrow window of opportunity for a ballot opened up here it never came.

It was correct of the NUM leaders not to be bounced into a ballot by the Tories, the reactionary press or by their allies in the Labour and trade union movement, who one-sidedly and sanctimoniously called for a ballot from the early days of the strike. These same people never called for a ballot about the use of the police and were quite happy to decide unilaterally without a ballot that the Tory 'right to work' was inapplicable to those workers who took action to defend their jobs.

The issue of whether or not a ballot was conducted was ultimately not responsible for the defeat of the strike. The working class, understanding the hypocrisy of the Tories, rallied in overwhelming numbers to support the miners, financially, industrially and practically helping to offset the almighty ruling class onslaught.

At each stage of the strike, Militant urged miners to adopt the strategy of appealing to the movement to put pressure on the tops of the unions to organise solidarity action. We also urged the NUM leaders and miners to call on the Left leaders in the unions to pursue a strategy independent of the right, such was the urgency of support needed for the miners.

How these tasks were approached during the strike was to become the crucial issue that ultimately all the Left leaders, unfortunately including Scargill, did not successfully measure up to.

NOTES

1   *Strike, 358 days that shook the nation*, Sunday Times Insight team, 1985, p57

2   Joe Owens, *Miners 1984-94, A Decade of endurance*, Polygon, Edinburgh 1994, p7

3   Strike, 358 that shook the nation, Sunday Times Insight team, Coronet 1985, p78

4   A ballot could have been called while workers were on strike – not just at work - and the union could have organised meetings away from management pressure at the pits in Nottingham – possibly organising transport etc – and allowing strikers to mix with non-strikers and persuade them of the case for action.

5   St John's, led by *Militant* supporters, was one of the six. It eventually closed in December 1985, two years later than the Coal Board had originally planned. The Lodge leadership and members continued to fight against the colliery closing for nine months after the strike and were seen as a model of resistance to closure at that time; conducting an independent public inquiry which proved that the pit was being closed for political reasons and not for uneconomic or geological reasons.

6   *Militant*, issue 692, 23 March 1984

7   Silver Birch was the nickname the media gave to Butcher as he travelled from coalfield to coalfield trying to organise strikebreaking activities.

NEVER HAVE SO FEW
OWED SO MUCH
TO SO MANY. *Alan Hardman*

THE TORY government had prepared for strikes like the miners by introducing anti-union laws and testing them out at the Warrington Stockport Messenger dispute.

There is some dispute among right-wing commentators about whether the Tories wanted the strike or not. Former chancellor Lawson claimed later that the cabinet didn't think that the miners would strike, given that it was approaching the end of winter and with all the contingency plans they had made. Nevertheless it was clear that Thatcher and her inner circle were quite prepared to face down the miners.

For the miners also, once the strike began, there was a realisation that to delay any further would only leave them in a worse position.

Thatcher, unlike some of her ministers, had a clear political perspective about the strike and its implications for the ruling class. For her this was an industrial version of the Falklands War which had to be pursued to the bitter end - no matter what the cost.

Hugo Young, in his biography of Thatcher claims that her preparations for the strike were a fairly rare example of Thatcher's capacity for strategic planning. *"She was not by heart a strategist... In the case of the miners, however, she had thought ahead. Tribal memories required it."* [1]

The miners were not the only example of Thatcher's 'strategic planning'. It was quite clear after the Tory climbdown over Liverpool city council in July 1984 – settling to avoid a second front developing alongside the miners – that she went away and prepared revenge. [2]

But Thatcher and the Tories, along with the majority of the capitalist class, did not initially feel confident about testing out their new anti-union laws further against the miners. Even when they did use the anti-union laws at a later stage, their enforcement of them did not seriously determine the outcome of the strike but were rather used to sap the effective organisation of the miners' union.

The Tories' class law

THATCHER MADE a political calculation that if the miners could be beaten it would clear the way for further attacks on the working class. This proved to be generally correct although the long-term legacy of the strike was increasing social division and bitterness against the Tories. Initially, because the miners had fought there was a shift to the left on many social issues - even if this wasn't immediately reflected in industrial or political struggles - something Thatcher and the Tories did not anticipate.

The unofficial strikes of check-in workers at Heathrow and the postal workers in 2003, have shown that once workers move en masse and remain united the anti-union laws can be swept aside with impunity.

Since the strike there has never been an example of the anti-union laws being used for anything other than effectively scaring the union leaders into policing their membership on behalf of the capitalist state. However, the anti-union laws are still a potential weapon that the capitalists can and will use if they think the balance of class forces is in their favour.

At the beginning of the strike the NCB did use the anti-union laws to get an injunction against flying pickets. But it consequently chose not to pursue the union for contempt of court when it was flagrantly ignored. This is something the NCB chairman of the time, Ian MacGregor, openly acknowledges in his autobiography.

Also, at different stages of the strike, other public-sector industries were instructed not to pursue injunctions against the NUM for fear of inflaming the situation to the point where other unions came out in sympathy.

Hugo Young points out how scared the Tories were of using their anti-union laws: *"Only later did the full measure of the deception become clear. A senior official at the Department of Employment gave me a graphic account of the calculations. British Steel in particular, had pressed hard to go to court. But government, at the highest level, was adamant that this should not happen.*

"The strategy, which had to be a political strategy, was to do nothing that might unite workers from steel, or the railways or the docks with the miners, and nothing that would undermine the commitment of around 25,000 miners, mainly in Nottinghamshire, to defy the union and carry on working." [3]

And also, according to Young, Thatcher personally intervened to give workers in public-sector industries better pay rises, in order to avoid a second front of strikes opening up. A leaked letter from a Downing Street private secretary revealed Thatcher's wishes. It *"agrees that BR* [the nationalised railways] *should increase its pay offer"* and *"accepts that the pay offer can be increased along the lines suggested."* [4]

Mass criminalisation

INSTEAD, THE main aspect of the law used against the miners was not the civil law contained in the anti-union legislation but a policy of mass criminalisation of the miners and their families. In every mining town and village those involved with the strike were charged en masse with criminal damage, riot, breach of the peace, assault and obstruction, to name a few.

From the early 1980s a distinct transfomation occured of Britain's police, traditionally viewed as the paternalistic Dixon of Dock Green local bobby, into a paramilitary force. This effectively began after 1981 riots in Brixton, London and Toxteth, Liverpool. At the same time there were the first attempts to ensure the

Solidarity - Food to Nottinghamshire striking miners, 25 November 1984
photo by Mark Salmon

creation of a national police force in all but name through widespread national co-ordination of the actions of the different area police forces.

Again, Hugo Young points out, the *"preparation of the police obliged the Home Office to [have] moved a very long way since 1981".* [5] The Police National Reporting Centre became a permanent facility after the 1981 riots in Liverpool, London and other parts of Britain.

Thatcher's deputy Lord Whitelaw said at the height of the miners' strike: *"If we hadn't had the Toxteth riots, I doubt if we could have dealt with Arthur Scargill."* [6]

All of these processes begun and tested out then have now gone much further. They have been used overwhelmingly against striking workers and anti-capitalist/anti-establishment protesters.

In effect, the whole strike was treated as a mass public order situation by the Tory government, with the law applied in a brutal class fashion. For the first time on the streets of Britain, methods that had been tested out in Northern Ireland were used – not against alleged terrorists (although Thatcher later equated miners with terrorists) but against working people trying to defend their jobs and their communities.

In the 1970s, Militant had warned, for example during the 1977 firefighters' strike where troops attempted to cover firefighters' duties, that the state forces were not neutral but would be used against the working class. At the time many on the Left disagreed, believing that Britain's police would not, even could not, behave like the police in Latin American dictatorships.

We warned that the police and other state forces were being prepared for an all-out confrontation with the working class.

Statistics could never fully convey the intimidation and brutality used by Thatcher's boot boys in blue but they can give some indicator of the way the law was applied to the miners, their families and supporters.

During the strike over 11,000 people were arrested and over 5,000 stood trial, with over 100 being jailed.[7] During the first nine months of the strike, 509 people were charged with unlawful assembly, and 137 were charged with riot - a figure higher than the total number found guilty of such charges in the previous three years; a period which included more riots in Britain (like those mentioned above) than had been experienced for decades.

The police were using the criminal law in the most blatant, shameful way to stop people getting into the coalfields and mount effective picketing. In the first 27 weeks of the strike 164,506 presumed pickets were prevented from entering Nottingham, according to the Chief Constable Charles McLachlan.[8]

Parts of Nottinghamshire, and Yorkshire, Scotland and Northumberland later in the dispute, became mini police states in all but name, as Thatcher's boot boys developed an overtly political role to drive the miners back to work.

Yet, throughout the strike, no police were charged in relation to complaints brought against them. In 1991 South Yorkshire police had to pay half a million pounds in damages to 39 miners arrested on 18 June 1984 at Orgreave. The miners sued the police for assault, wrongful arrest, malicious prosecution and false imprisonment after their original trial for riot humiliatingly collapsed in 1985.

From early on in the strike up to 8,000 police a day were being mobilised to stop miners reaching picket lines. These police were drawn from 41 of Britain's 43 police forces. Over 20,000 police in all were deployed during the 12 months of the strike. Militant reported on 27 April 1984 that the cost of policing the dispute had reached £1.5 million a day.

At that stage secondary picketing had lost its legal immunity in the first batch of anti-union laws introduced by Thatcher and the Tories, although it was not a criminal activity the police proceeded to treat it as such.

The police all the time claimed that they were acting within the realm of *"operational decisions"* but it was apparent from early on that the Tory government was pulling the strings. They used a national security committee set up in 1972 after the defeat Heath's Tory government suffered at the hands of the miners. This was later renamed the civil contingencies committee.

Incredibly, the New Labour government is looking to extend their civil contingency powers after the successes of the postal workers in defying the anti-union laws and carrying out effective 'illegal' secondary picketing and solidarity action which forced Royal Mail managers to retreat.

Ruling class prepares for civil war

THROUGHOUT THE 1970s the ruling class was fearful of the radicalised working class moving leftwards and posing a direct threat to the continued existence of their precious capitalist system of wealth and privilege.

In 1977, Sir Robert Mark, a former head of the Metropolitan Police, fulminated about what he saw as the most serious threat to society: *"I do not think that what we call 'crimes of violence' are anything like as severe a threat to the maintenance of tranquility in this country as the tendency to use violence to achieve political or industrial ends. As far as I am concerned that is the worst crime in the book. I think it is worse than murder."* [9]

However, although the police were much better prepared than in 1972 or 1974, the way they were used by the Tories in 1984 was always a risky strategy.

The Guardian in January 1995 reported that police officers felt *"betrayed by the Thatcher government and badly led by some senior officers during the 1984-85 miners' strike, according to an official history of the Police Federation".*

The report goes on to say that *"the Federation leaders and probably the great majority of chief officers would have been shocked had they discovered that there had been secret political collusion between MacGregor, Thatcher and others".* It points out that the police National Reporting Centre, which co-ordinated police action during the strike, was set up on the instructions of central government and not at senior officers' request as was claimed at the time.

Ultimately, it was still the political factors that were decisive. The state and all its forces will prove powerless in the face of united action by key sections of workers.

The coercive apparatus of the state remains effective only while the working class remains unconscious of its own power.

The main sense in which Marxists use the term 'state' is to describe the institutions by which class rule is maintained. We live in a class society where the ruling class does not represent the interests of the whole population, where a minority maintains its power and privileges by exploiting the majority.

They do this partly though their control of ideas, for example, through their ownership of the mass media, their general control of education and other institutions. They try to persuade people that their system is the only and best way of organising society.

But when their ideas and system clash with the interests of working-class people, as they did in the miners' strike, then the ruling class use the police, the courts, the law and sometimes the army to defend their profits and power.

They have specifically developed their special apparatus to ensure that their class rule continues. The core of the state, the part which it falls back on to ensure its rule when all else fails, is the repressive apparatus - the police, the army, the courts and the various intelligence agencies like MI5. (Friedrich Engels, Karl Marx's revolutionary co-thinker, described the state as ultimately being *"a body of armed men"*).

Carrying through the transition to a socialist society inevitably includes major strategic and tactical problems in defeating these agencies which exist to defend capitalist class rule.

There were a few key periods when the powers of the state, including the police and, covertly, the army, were used to try and undermine the strike; namely the first two months of attempts to picket out the Nottinghamshire and Midlands miners, secondly the flashpoint of Orgreave during May and June and then during the back-to-work movement from August onwards. During this latter period whole areas of Yorkshire, Durham and Scotland were put under siege by the police and scenes of the most appalling, indiscriminate brutality ensued. Areas like Fitzwilliam in Yorkshire and Easington in Durham were effectively sealed off to the outside world for days while the police ran amok. Militant carried some vivid eyewitness reports from these communities.[10]

These events showed the full brutality of the state when its rule is challenged and at the same time showed the potential power of the working class if harnessed, no matter what repressive state forces are thrown at it.

However, these occasions demonstrate that in what was no ordinary strike the 'ordinary' past tactics of mass picketing would also not be enough. More would have to be done in the form of solidarity action from the wider working class.

If the strategy and tactics of the miners' leaders had developed away from a reliance on mass picketing and bureacratic deals with the trade union leaders, then no matter what state forces were thrown against the miners the strike could have reached a speedier and successful conclusion.

As we shall see later, despite the lopsided civil war that was conducted against the miners using all the forces of the state that Thatcher could reasonably use without provoking an insurrection, the miners' resolve to win remained undaunted. This iron will caused huge cracks to open up in the capitalist class and Tory government in July and from September to October 1984, as the prospect of other unions taking strike action appeared imminent.

Events in Notts

HOWEVER, BY the latter part of May it was clear that the police action had been decisive in effectively stopping mass picketing in Notts and the prospect of solidarity action in defence of the miners' right to carry out secondary picketing was not yet forthcoming.

At that time an editorial in Militant argued for a change of tack. Arguing that, unfortunately, *"divisions were entrenched by the way the rolling strike began in March"*, it said: *"The fact remains that Notts have yet to be thoroughly **convinced** of the need for a national strike over jobs".*[11] [Emphasis in original]

It argued then for an attempt to get into the Lion's Den another way by trying official mass leafletting in Notts and approaching working miners about arranging meetings to discuss the issues, no matter how high feelings had got by that stage.

It argued for flying squads of canvassers who would take nothing for granted and it concluded: *"If the Notts miners could be won over and brought out, a total British coalfield strike would get ten or a hundred times more support even than has already been shown."*[12]

Notts was a key coalfield. Clearly if it came out there would not be enough coal stocks for the Tory government to get through the winter without entering a state of emergency like Heath's in 1974.

Arrest at Easington Village, County Durham
photo by Keith Pattison

The very next week Militant carried an exclusive report that, even at this relatively early stage, there was a fear amongst the CEGB and government of coal stocks running dangerously low. It reported that the CEGB had shut down or curtailed the power at 55 of the country's 57 coal powered fire stations. Only two power stations in the East Midlands - High Markham and West Burton - were operating at more than 50% capacity.

In Yorkshire, coal stock was shrinking by 140,000 tonnes per week since the start of the strike according to an inside source, a North-East Yorkshire power worker.

However, even if the stations were only getting a quarter of their supply it was possible for the stations to continue for a number of months - albeit at dangerous levels on occasions. As well as stopping the coal coming out of Nottingham, the key task was for the NUM to effectively picket out the large oil and coal burning power stations.

However, another turn of events focussed miners' leader Arthur Scargill to concentrate on stopping coal going into steelworks.

NOTES

1   Hugo Young, *One of Us*, 1993 Pan Books, p367
2   Contrary to some ultra-left sects' claims, Liverpool in itself was not the key dispute that could have delivered the solidarity to help the miners win their struggle. It would have been impossible for the council leadership to keep the Liverpool struggle at full tilt when the Tories were offering a settlement. Such a light-minded approach could have rebounded on them. For more details see *Liverpool the City that Dared to Fight* by Tony Mulhearn and Peter Taaffe
3   Hugo Young, *One of Us*, 1993 Pan Books, p370
4   ibid, p371
5   ibid, p368
6   ibid p368
7   One *Militant* miner, Nick Platteck, was jailed for breaking a police order by going for a pint of milk within half a mile of his pit.
8   *Strike, 358 days that shook the nation*, Sunday Times Insight team, p69
9   Quoted in an article by Lynn Walsh on police strategy, *Militant* issue 695, p5
10 Detailed eyewitness accounts of the events at Fitzwilliam were carried in *Militant* issue 708
11 *Militant* issue 700, 18 May 1984
12 ibid

One of many victims - James O'Brian - acquitted of riot in the Orgreave trial. He ended up in hospital after been assulted by riot police. His case was one of those featured in Channel Four's 'The Battle for Orgreave' which revealed - years later - the facts of the day this photo was taken, 19 June 1984

photo by Sheffield Newspapers

"You have been fighting the legions of Hell"
Miners' leader AJ Cook to striking miners in 1926

THE PIVOTAL showdown between the state and the miners was at Orgreave coking works, just south of Sheffield, between 23 May and 18 June 1984. There were many turning points in the ebbs and flows of the battle during the 358 days of its duration, where the initiative shifted from one side to the other. The situation in Nottinghamshire at the start of the strike; the negotiations in July and September, the back-to-work movement from late August onwards, the NACODS ballot in September-October and the sequestration of the South Wales and national NUM funds were all crucial stages.

Orgreave, above others, represented a big defeat for the idea that mass picketing alone could effectively win the strike. At Orgreave all the elements of the Tory plan outlined in the Ridley Report came into play.

And there appears fairly conclusive circumstantial evidence that although Orgreave was not the 'honey trap' some Tories claim, it was nevertheless seen as an opportunity for the full brutality of the state to be unleashed, to serve as a warning to all workers.

At the time many miners felt uneasy about how simple it was to get to Orgreave on the crucial days of mass picketing - especially the 6th and 18th June. However, if it was a cunning plan designed to lure the miners in to a trap, then it came perilously close to unravelling.

"The chief constable of Yorkshire later conceded that that if mass picketing had continued after 18 June, the police would have had difficulty keeping the plant open." [1]

The police riot

Despite the incredible odds stacked against the miners at Orgreave – particularly on 6th and 18th June – the brutality of the police sent shockwaves around the world and brought an increase of public sympathy towards the miners and their supporters.

Civil rights organisation Liberty described the unprecedented viciousness that day: *"There was a riot. But it was a police riot."* [2]

There are many lessons from Orgreave to be reviewed and learned from to prepare for future workers' struggles. Inevitably, at some big battle in the future the state will look to unleash similar tactics attempting to break the morale of striking workers.

The miners were by that time better prepared than any other group of workers could have been for the battle of Orgreave. The events at the coking works did effectively represent a military-type battle and the miners were as well drilled and as disciplined as any 'army' in their situation could be.

But looked at overall, you draw the conclusion that the miners' leaders – wittingly or unwittingly – chose the wrong issue and wrong battleground at Orgreave.

Confusion over steel blockade

FROM EARLY in the strike there had been much confusion about the supply of coking coal to steel plants. These plants needed a certain amount of coal for 'care and maintenance' so blast furnaces would not crack and be put out of commission.

Although such supplies had been maintained in 1972 and 1974, that was done in a completely solid strike where miners effectively exercised workers' control over the movement of coal. Where this was not adhered to through agreement with other unions, the NUM provided flying pickets to stop coal being transported.

In 1972 the closure of Saltley depot in Birmingham by Arthur Scargill's flying pickets proved a decisive moment, which led the miners to a clear victory.

But the memory of Saltley and the workers' power it displayed was a major element in the Tories' plans for 1984. Both sides – Arthur Scargill and Margaret Thatcher – knew that another attempt at a 'Saltley' could develop.[3]

Different factors were at play in 1984, which meant the NUM did not have the same control over the movement of coal. Not least of these was Nottinghamshire's working and providing extra coal for steel and power plants.

Also, the use of non-union haulage drivers who would cross picket lines allowed supplies to get into steelworks. Last but not least, were the deals done by area NUM leaders, which provided more coal than was needed for just keeping the blast furnaces hot enough for continued future operation.

In May, after months of a lack of national direction on the issue, Scargill decided it was time to seal up the steel plants by increasing mass picketing. Militant did not disagree with this, as the British Steel Corporation – aided and abetted by the leadership of the ISTC, such as Bill Sirs – were clearly getting away with strike-breaking.

Many of our miners and supporters in South Wales participated in the mass pickets at Port Talbot, which were explosive and bitter on occasions. Similarly, Militant miners in Scotland participated in the huge struggles at Ravenscraig.

Hundreds of Militant members were involved at Orgreave, even though many had uneasy misgivings about what was likely to be unleashed. However, we also argued that building links with power workers and picketing of power plants would prove more effective than concentrating on the steelworks. We argued this for a number of reasons.

Orgreave – another Saltley?

MOST OF the steelworks in Britain are situated near deep-water ports for coal and ore to be unloaded. During the strike huge amounts of coal were imported into the nearby ports to service Port Talbot, Llanwern and Ravenscraig. The only site that was relatively landlocked was Scunthorpe in Lincolnshire, which was supplied with coking coal from Orgreave, 40 miles further inland.

Port Talbot, supplied much coal for Llanwern. Non-union haulage firms, as well as lorries driven by union drivers were taking coal through mass picket lines there aided by a heavy police presence.[4]

At Port Talbot a week of pitched battles took place outside the plant as the lorries came out. There were also other innovative tactics like a convoy of miners' cars trying to block off the coal lorries on the M4 motorway.

But it was clear such action was not going to quickly stop the supplies getting through. Many thousands more pickets were needed and even then it was not guaranteed that it would be successful.

Scargill thought he saw his opportunity for another Saltley at Orgreave. It was not wrong to look for such an opportunity, particularly to boost the strikers in what was shaping up to be a long war. Nevertheless, the strategy at Orgreave was not adequately thought through.

And whilst the savage beatings inflicted upon the miners and their supporters on 6 June provoked uproar and, if anything, made most miners more determined than ever not to give in, the ultimate defeat at Orgreave after 18 June caused many to question whether or not mass picketing could now achieve anything effective.

Some drew conclusions in a pessimistic one-sided way. Kim Howells was among the first to throw the baby out with the bathwater and denounce mass picketing. Responding to criticism about the increasing number of scab lorries going into Port Talbot and Llanwern steel works later on in the strike Howells said: *"Challenging lines of single-minded and well-equipped policemen... had already been tried in most spectacular fashion at Orgreave... it never succeeded in stopping a single lorry nor a scab and taught us in South Wales a good deal about what to do to win friends and influence people during industrial disputes."*[5]

Howells wrote a paper on co-ordinating the strike after this which was dismissed by Scargilll. From then on these two, trained in the same Communist stable, became bitter enemies.

What Howells was effectively proposing, along with some other leading lights in the South Wales NUM, was scaling down picketing – something opposed by Militant supporters in the South Wales NUM.

However, Militant miners in South Wales and other areas also had a clear alternative strategy of how to build secondary solidarity action from below, bypassing the failed official attempts at the top, which had produced nothing of any effectiveness.

The end of mass picketing?

HOWELLS WAS in a sense partly right, although we would not draw the same conclusions as he would. Orgreave was a big failure for the idea particularly beloved of groups like the SWP, that mass picketing in itself can be enough to win industrial disputes *(see chapter 8)*.

Mass picketing can be an important part of any industrial dispute. Thatcher's anti-union laws exist on the statute book to this day, supposedly limiting the number of pickets on a picket line to six and prohibiting secondary picketing. And, workers have increasingly shown themselves to be prepared to disregard these laws. In any current dispute the numbers picketing almost always amount to dozens, if not hundreds, and the police and government have not been able to act.

For picketing to be effective it is not just a matter of numbers; there has to be a consciousness among all workers not to cross picket lines. Also, the workers who are on strike have to have the economic muscle to shut down a workplace in a way that can force the bosses to back down.

During the postal workers' dispute in 2003, management tried to isolate the strikers but because of the bosses' miscalculations and the workers' burning anger, the strike was actually spreading causing huge financial damage to Royal Mail – somewhere in the region of £50 million to £100 million.

At Orgreave in 1984 the signs for similar effective action were not as propitious. Electricity rather than Steel was the biggest customer for coal in 1984 – burning 81.8 million tonnes in 1983. Closing the generating stations or causing power cuts would have been far and away the most effective tactic. However, there were huge stocks at power stations and a mild spring and early summer meant that large-scale picketing would not have been seen by the national leadership as a realistic target – at least not until the autumn – although this was argued against by many Militant miners who were building up good links with rank-and-file power workers.

Undoubtedly, Arthur Scargill and the national NUM leadership would have been rightly wary of relying on the leaders of the power workers' unions. These were extreme right-wingers in the pockets of Thatcher - such as Gavin Laird of the engineers, John Lyons of the power managers and Eric Hammond of the electricians, who played a notorious role as a strikebreaker in the 1986 Wapping dispute.[6]

Steel in contrast was not as big a prize as it was portrayed by Arthur Scargill at the time; it only consumed 4.3 million tonnes for its blast furnaces in 1983-84.

Although there had been agreement from the end of March to pinpoint supplies going into steelworks, the compromise deals reached by area leaders had undermined the prospect of it having any effect.

NUM leaders like Mick McGahey in Scotland had fought alongside members of the Scottish Tory Party and the Church of Scotland for years in a broad, cross-class alliance – a popular front campaign - claiming it was in Scotland's 'national' interest rather than the interests of the Scottish working class to keep Ravenscraig near Motherwell open *(see chapter 8)*.

Area leaders fudge the issue

BY THE end of April, the two trainloads a day McGahey had agreed to go into Ravenscraig had been stretched to such lengths by management that extra locomotives were needed to haul the trucks. Then the NUM and NUR announced they would only allow one train delivery a day.

British Steel's response was to increase the coal being driven in by cowboy operators, offering drivers £50-£80 a day (a substantial amount at the time) and increasing the tonnage going into the plant. McGahey's response was to try and hammer out a new two-train formula, which allowed 18,000 tonnes a week for the plant – three times the minimum needed to keep the furnaces alight.

Ravenscraig, Llanwern and Port Talbot being close to deep-water ports were not seen as good options for effective blockades. Scunthorpe though looked different, being more landlocked and dependent on domestic rather than foreign coal supplies. Its iron ore also came in from Immingham on the Humber, which was to cause further problems after the battle of Orgreave when the dockers came out on strike.

Initially, management at Scunthorpe said they were happy with the supplies of coal they were receiving and did not require any coke from Orgreave. However, seeing what other plants were getting away with and that steel production at the plant had dropped by nearly 25% they changed policy.

Then management used a problem with one of the blast furnaces to try and extract more concessions from the NUM, which were refused.

At first, pickets had some success, with relatively small numbers, in blockading Scunthorpe. But soon, cowboy drivers brought in new supplies from Flixborough on the river Trent.

Then policing was intensified at both Orgreave and Scunthorpe to allow convoys of lorries to Scunthorpe. Although the police presence was being stepped up, there were times when pickets had caught police on the hop.

Also, 300 transport union members in Scunthorpe were furious at the use of non-union labour and tried to mount their own picket line, which was viciously broken up by police. By the time of the spring bank holiday Arthur Scargill had become personally involved, believing that a mass blockade of Orgreave under his charge could become a Saltley Mark II.

In many TV, radio and press interviews of the time he built up the prospects around Orgreave implying that closing the plant would succeed because no force in the land could prevent a determined, well organised mass picket from shutting down a designated, factory, plant or workplace.

Unfortunately, given the forces stacked against the miners at Orgreave, despite their incredible bravery and heroism, Scargill's optimism was to prove badly misplaced.

But his statements ensured that the attempt to blockade Scunthorpe through a mass picket of the Orgreave coking works 40 miles away was set to become a crucial battle to see if picketing could close a steelworks.

The battlegrounds of Orgreave

THE BATTLE for Orgreave dominated the strike for nearly four weeks from 23 May to 18 June and the coverage of it swamped many of the nightly news bulletins at the time.

One of those news bulletins became infamous for swapping round the actual sequence of events to show miners attacking police when an inquiry later revealed that it was the other way round.

On the most momentous days of battle, around 10,000 miners were confronted with 4,000-5,000 police – most of them equipped for paramilitary style conflict – along with hundreds of police 'Cossacks' on horses and dozens of police dogs that were unleashed by their handlers.

If any point in the strike represented graphically that there was a virtual civil war raging in the heart of Britain then it was Orgreave.

Daily news bulletins showed miners with wounds and blood streaming down their faces. One famous picture shows Lesley Boulton from a women's support group about to be viciously truncheoned by a police outrider (this book's front cover image). Lesley later spoke to Militant about her experience.[7]

The Chief Police Constable at Orgreave, Peter Wright, bluntly outlined what was at stake: *"Whatever resources were needed would be provided. It was I who decided that Orgreave should stay open. I was well aware that if the pickets pulled it off at Orgreave they would move on and try it elsewhere."* [8]

NCB chairman MacGregor recalls how he (and probably Thatcher as well) viewed Orgreave: *"From the NCB's point of view we had been forced by competition from foreign sources for some years to sell the coal from Cortonwood and the other pits at a price far lower than it cost us to produce. So when Arthur Scargill decided that this was going to be the battle of Saltley 1984 – it wasn't really in the long run a critical matter to us whether he won or lost.*

"If he won and Orgreave and Scunthorpe were shut, then all the NCB would have lost would have been the obligation to supply some high-cost production from a pit which we would now have an even better reason for shutting down. If he lost, then clearly, since he chose the site, the day and the weapons for the pitched battle, then it would be an enormous blow to his confidence and credibility. Either way it would keep his army out of Nottingham." [9]

Whilst there is a large dose of post-strike bravado in MacGregor's statement it is very likely that such thoughts were being bandied around in the highest circles of the NCB and government.

On a number of occasions it looked like they were going to be left with egg on their faces. Even if strategically Orgreave wasn't all that important for them, a victory for the miners at Orgreave would have represented a blow to the ruling class around Thatcher who wanted to win the strike, whatever it cost.

It was not long after the unprecedented violence at Orgreave, provoked by the police, that Thatcher referred to the miners as the "Enemy Within", confirming the military and political dimension she attached to the miners' strike. This was an insult she applied to the Militant as well.

Once started, Orgreave was a battle that neither side could afford to lose.

Thatcher and the Tories threw everything at it: state forces; propaganda; political pressure on the Labour and trade union leaders and the full force of the legal system against arrested miners.

Police 'gladiators' were instructed from early on by police officers with loudhailers to *"take prisoners"*.[10] In reply the miners mobilised the biggest most determined pickets this country has ever seen.

However, despite the presence of many hundreds if not thousands of trade unionists from other unions and supporters from the support groups, ten thousand miners were not enough to resist a state onslaught of this scale. Unfortunately, despite Arthur Scargill saying correctly that the scenes were reminiscent of the police dictatorships of Latin America, he did not make a call for the wider union movement to take action to defend the miners at Orgreave.

If he had called for a 24-hour general strike of supporting unions – with or without the backing of the TUC – and on that day called for mass picket of a hundred thousand or more to show solidarity with the miners at Orgreave then matters could have taken a different turn.

Again, regretably, Scargill and the NUM leaders did not display the breadth of vision to mobilise that level of active mass support, and a huge opportunity to draw in the wider working class en masse in solidarity action went begging.

A new strategy needed

ORGREAVE REPRESENTED a big setback, which emboldened the government to be more provocative in its attacks on the miners. Until then Thatcher and the Tories had tried to maintain the pretence that this was an industrial dispute over pit closures from which they remained aloof. Of course everyone could see Thatcher pulling the strings behind the scenes.

Yet, the miners' steadfast refusal to buckle and their willingness to defend their jobs and their union at all costs, allowed more opportunities for victory to present themselves: the dockers' strike, the NACODS ballot and also a growing shortage of coal for the power industry in the autumn were all going to give Thatcher's government further wobbles.

But, the defeat at Orgreave clearly put the idea of winning the strike through picketing alone on the back foot. Emboldened NCB area managers began the drive to get a small section of demoralised strikers back to work to tie up pickets in their own home areas, rather than being able to effectively picket power stations or raise funds and build wider solidarity.

From Orgreave onwards right-wing union and Labour leaders' support for the strike – always equivocal at best – began to get more critical and echoed the propaganda of the Tories.

However, a lesson to be drawn after Orgreave was that a new strategy was needed: a strategy to build pressure on the union leaders – both Left and right – from below.

NOTES

1 *The Enemy Within*, Seumas Milne, Verso, London 1994, p271

2 *Guardian*, 20 June 1991

3 South Wales NUM research officer Kim Howells sent pickets to Saltley in March 1984 only for them to discover it had been shut in 1982

4 These drivers were members of the TGWU which was dominated in Wales by right-winger George Wright who spent more of his time during the strike witch-hunting *Militant* supporters than organising to assist the miners

5 *Digging Deeper*, Huw Benyon (editor) London 1985, p145

6 Chapter 7 on the role of the union leaders deals with this in more detail

7 Carried in *Militant* issue 709

8 *Strike, 358 days that shook the nation*, Sunday Times Insight team, Coronet 1985, p101

9 *The Enemies Within*, Ian MacGregor with Rodney Tyler, Fontana 1985, p207

10 *Strike, 358 days that shook the nation*, Sunday Times Insight team, Coronet, London 1985, p88

WHAT FORCE OR GUILE COULD NOT SUBDUE IS WROUGHT NOW BY A COWARD FEW. — ROBBIE BURNS

Neil Kinnock (left) and TUC leader Morman Willis tun their backs on the miners.

SOME UNION leaders knew the high stakes that a showdown with Thatcher involved. Jim Slater, leader of the National Union of Seafarers, said at the start of the strike: *"We can't afford to let the miners lose this strike. It would put us back to 1926. And it is doubtful if we would ever recover"*[1] But, the Left leaders looked on almost powerless as the forces of the state were unleashed on the miners and as the strike was undermined by the right-wing union leaders. The TUC, controlled by the right wing, did not even discuss the miners' strike until August. When, eventually it did become involved, after the TUC Congress in September, it was to conduct a lamentable exercise in procrastination and deceit.

The need to organise effective solidarity action showed, unfortunately, the incapacity of even the best union leaders to do so. Even where unions were controlled by Left leaders who may have genuinely wanted to assist the miners they seemed to lack the ideas or means to achieve it.

Most Left leaders genuinely did not want the miners to lose, regardless of how they felt towards Arthur Scargill or the other miners' leaders. However, the Left union leaders, even the NUM as we have seen, had not prepared sufficiently – either politically or organisationally – for the inevitable showdown with Thatcher.

Certainly amongst a layer of activists from early on in the strike, there was a concern that the NUM leaders (and the Left leaders of other unions) were refighting the battles of the 1970s. In using the same tactics and strategy, rather than facing up to the different character of this struggle, particularly as the strike escalated and stretched into a marathon struggle, they showed themselves incapable of inspiring the broad mass of trade unionists who wanted to act alongside the miners.

Many of the bigger unions in 1984 were in words more to the Left and with a better degree of organisation at shop steward level than exists today, even with the recent rise of the 'awkward squad' (although even then a drift to the right was becoming evident).

So how, then, could they not deliver the solidarity action that was needed – particularly given the huge wave of support for the miners that developed amongst the organised working class and society generally?

Ultimately, the Left had lost touch with the rank and file and lacked the confidence to show the decisive leadership required. They did not have the strategic and tactical understanding necessary to take the strike forward at key stages. And they did not have the willingness to struggle and go to the end that the rank-and-file miners showed during the strike.

In particular, the Left union leaders had not built Broad Lefts, with links to every level of the rank and file, capable of delivering the effective action needed to win the

Miners' food convoy donated by printworkers on their way to Barnsley, 2 August 1984
photo by John Smith

miners' strike, in their own unions. Also, they had not helped to build strong Left currents in the right-wing unions which could have transformed those unions during the course of the strike.

A Broad Left is a body within a union, which brings all the best Left activists together from every level of the union. When working effectively a Broad Left can co-ordinate and defeat right-wing ideas in the union and act as a transmission belt between the top and bottom of the union in a way which holds the leadership genuinely to account.

Even in the NUM, many of the Left leaders, with a few exceptions, were found wanting. Had there been an open rank-and-file based Broad Left in the NUM before the strike started, especially involving people in Nottingham, then many aspects of the strike would not have developed in such a complicated fashion.

Instead, the NUM Broad Left was a semi-secret body of 50 senior full-time officials, even though the Left had a 13-11 majority on the NEC from Scargill's election as president. Only later in the strike were there attempts to bring in new blood from the rank and file and make it more open, but it was too little too late.

Also, if the miners and other Left unions had assisted by example and practical guidance in building Broad Lefts in other unions, especially the power workers, these could have challenged the corrupt right-wing leadership in those unions. That would have made solidarity action from below - bypassing the obstruction of the right-wing national union leaders - much easier to build.

The Left had control of the NUM at a national level and in most of the key areas. The majority of the rank-and-file miners, as was shown during the strike, were well to the Left in terms of industrial militancy and political consciousness.

But the majority of miners were not involved in the decision making about how the strike would develop.

The Left leadership in the areas were a hybrid mixture of long-standing Communist Party and Labour Lefts who had long controlled their areas throughout periods of right-wing dominance in the NUM and a newer Left who had come to prominence in the 1970s' strikes.

They had become accustomed to a way of working with the nationalised coal board management which involved arriving at 'consensus' decisions, often decided by only a small layer of union officials. That method of working was something they replicated in their running of the NUM and the strike.

The Left had developed as a small tightly organised, even secretive Broad Left inside the NUM in the days of right-wing domination. No Left leaders had attempted to build a genuine mass Broad Left that involved the rank and file of the union. Often, left-wing officials at national and local level were excluded from the Broad Left.

Under pressure

DURING THE strike a new generation of Left leaders began to come forward in the NUM and other unions. If the strike had been successful, along with the successful struggle in 1984 of the Militant-led Liverpool city council, this would have undoubtedly consolidated a huge shift to the Left in most unions and probably inside the Labour Party also.

This was something some union leaders and especially Labour leader Neil Kinnock did not want. The idea that militancy could bring results was something that would put them under enormous pressure and, as noted earlier, the majority of the leadership of the labour movement were moving rightwards after Labour's 1983 election defeat.

In contrast, Arthur Scargill was different to many of the NUM Left leadership and the other Left leaders in the unions. He undoubtedly had no intention of selling his membership or working-class people short.

During the strike and since Scargill has shown an unyielding defiance of the capitalist system and has not – unlike many of the strike's leading figures – renounced his past or the strike.

But, Scargill also often operated in isolation, lacking confidence in the people around him and inevitably making avoidable mistakes.

This partly stemmed from his initial membership of the Young Communist League and association with Stalinist CP industrial organisers, which encouraged a top-down approach to organising. And although he was very effective in inspiring the rank and file of the NUM, the way in which the NUM Left was organised did not bring in the best of the new generation at key stages in the strike when the old Left began to act as a brake on the struggle.

Also, on certain key issues, he placed too great an emphasis on one-off actions like the mass pickets at Orgreave. And his advocacy of the NUM's political and financial links to Stalinist regimes like the Soviet Union and one-party states caused certain problems later on in the strike, when the press conducted a witch-hunt relating to the NUM's finances after Roger Windsor visited Libya (without Scargill's knowledge).

But, the right wing's claim that the strike was all about Scargill's 'character' and that his belligerent stance was solely responsible for calling out over 150,000 miners on strike for a year and leading them to defeat was nonsense.

The miners' strike of 1984-85 was a defensive struggle and of a different charac-ter to an offensive struggle on pay. It is likely that the miners' strike of 1984-85 would have developed along relatively similar lines, regardless of whether or not Arthur Scargill was NUM leader,.

Indeed, Scargill and the majority of the NUM leaders, while not shying away from the fight to defend their industry, clearly approached the start of the strike cautiously in 1984 – particularly having lost two national ballots over strike action on pay.

The strike started spontaneously from below. But – like the unofficial action by the postal workers in 2003, which was triggered off by all manner of grievances – it nevertheless reflected the rank and file being to the left of the leadership in understanding the necessary response to the underlying crisis in the coal industry and the Thatcher government's desire to see off the miners.

More detailed evidence emerging since the strike indicates that top NUM leaders were not as committed or prepared as the rank and file for a long, bitter strike.

The rank and file miner, like the leadership of the Tory Party, understood the full significance of the dispute from its start. It was a battle to the finish where the wider layers of the working class needed to be drawn in to support the miners.

NUM members had enormous trust and confidence in their leadership to ensure such support would materialise.

Arthur Scargill and the NUM leadership did attempt to get solidarity action from other trade unions but generally it was restricted to contacts at the top of the unions, where the Left leaders were unsure or incapable of delivering and the right wing consciously sabotaged any prospect of effective action.

Had the NUM leaders developed contacts before the strike between miners, railworkers, steelworkers, and power workers at a rank-and-file level, as well as at the tops of the unions where possible, then even in the most right-wing-led unions a movement of effective solidarity action could have developed.

Indeed, heroic acts of 'illegal' secondary solidarity action occurred on a widespread basis. But, however much heroism was shown by individual workers the Left leaders did not build on the example these workers showed.

And in the right-wing unions every time action looked possible the national leadership consciously undermined it. The NUM leaders had not found or developed sufficient channels amongst the rank and file to reverse this sabotage.

Some union leaders openly sabotaged the strike from the beginning. Bill Sirs (later knighted for his services to capitalism), general secretary of the ISTC, made it clear early on that, despite the existence of a Triple Alliance of railworkers, steelworkers and miners (rechristened the Cripple Alliance because of its ineffectiveness under fire), he would not deliver solidarity action for the miners; even though miners had shown solidarity with steelworkers in their 13-week strike in 1980.

Eighteen weeks into the strike, with many miners' families already facing severe difficulties, the TUC's Steel Committee voted against any action which would cut steel production during the strike.

While the Militant poster argues the case for unity, Kinnock (centre) was busy doing the opposite *photo by Militant*

This flew in the face of the mood of ordinary steelworkers, such as those at Llanwern in South Wales who were collecting £2,000 a week for the striking miners.

Right wing break ranks

ON 29 March, the rail, road, transport and seafarers' unions called on their members to block all movements of coal (a call they did not sufficiently enforce). Within 24 hours, Sirs had broken ranks and accused the miners of threatening his members' jobs and said he would not see his members "sacrificed on someone else's altar." This was from a man who had misled his members to a bitter inglorious defeat in 1980, which led to over 70,000 steelworkers being sacked by British Steel.

To reinforce the point Sirs and his executive agreed that ISTC *"would handle fuel supplies, 'scab' or otherwise, from any source that presented itself"*. [2]

Steelworkers were understandably concerned about losing their jobs given the contracting worldwide demand for steel and the savage job losses their industry had suffered. Had any of the furnaces cracked and collapsed because their temperature dropped too far then inevitably, given that BSC had announced it wanted further cuts in capacity, they feared it would mean the closure of one or more of the big steel plants.

In many strikes 'emergency cover' of one kind or another is required to ensure that workers' interests are protected. Providing coking coal for steelworks at a sufficient level on a 'care and maintenance' basis to ensure the plants were not closed down was a legitimate concession, provided it was at a level that did not allow production to effectively continue or even increase.

Unfortunately, rather than trying to undercut any anxieties amongst rank-and-file steelworkers from below, the miners' leaders at area level made many compromises allowing coking coal to go into steelworks to prevent the furnaces from collapsing, which reinforced Sirs' argument.

Local NUM leaders were inconsistently providing extra help for the steelworks in their own areas, in fudged agreements, which could not be sustained or be effective during a long strike. At a later stage this brought them into conflict with Scargill's plans, which rigidly wanted to stop all coal deliveries into steelworks.

Mass pickets at steelworks were then necessary during the strike because of the criminal strikebreaking of the ISTC leadership. Had a Left leadership controlled the ISTC, then undoubtedly steelworkers themselves through their union would have policed agreements and miners would have been freed to picket power plants and build solidarity in other areas.

The right-wing leaders of the unions in the power industry, John Lyons of the power engineers' union and Eric Hammond of the electricians union, EEPTU, initially used the lack of a national ballot as an excuse for their inaction.

By the time of the TUC Congress in September, it was clear that whatever resolutions were passed they were going to openly sabotage any attempts to assist the miners.

Eric Hammond was booed when he said the TUC's pledges, which were passed overwhelmingly, were *"dishonest and deficient."* John Lyons of the power engineers was even more brutal about the meaninglessness of the TUC's decisions: *"We will not do it. Our members will not do it. I predict that other workers in the industry will not do it."*[3]

As treacherous as these statements were, they were an accurate reflection of the right wing of the TUC's inability to deliver support. John Monks, later to become TUC general secretary reported to the TUC seven weeks after their Congress resolutions supporting the miners on 7 November that *"union efforts to block the vital oil supplies had 'little discernible effect'. That there was little likelihood of 'crucial fuel shortages at the generating stations' [and] that in the absence of any further talks scheduled between the main parties 'prospects for an early settlement of the dispute are remote'."*[4]

Regrettably the Left leadership of the NUM and other unions did not adequately come up with a strategy to assist the Left and overcome the sabotage of the right wing.

Another opportunity was to present itself in September for bringing about a miners' victory – the NACODS strike ballot. In the meantime, how were the different sections of the Left responding to the challenges of this testing dispute?

NOTES

1   *Strike, 385 days that shook the nation,* Sunday Times Insight Team, p75
2   ibid, p85
3   ibid, p146
4   ibid, p22.

Miners lobby the 1984 TUC Conference, Brighton
photo by Militant

chapter 8 **Militant and the role of the Left**

N THE pages of the Militant every week during the strike you would have found article after article showing the tremendous solidarity organised for the miners. At the same time, in many of the articles we outlined how this could be used to deliver more than just cash and sympathy – as important as they were.

In the pages of the paper were many articles showing where workers had taken the initiative in support of the miners – often risking the sack or victimisation.

Militant supporters also did as much as we could in many other ways, given our forces at the time. One of the first conferences in defence of the miners was the Militant-led Broad Left Organising Committee (BLOC) conference on 24 March 1984 in Sheffield. This was attended by over 2,200 trade unionists including over 100 miners (60 of whom were official delegates), contained in a main hall and two overflow meetings to hear Tony Benn MP and leading trade unionists speak. Over 500 people had to be turned away from the conference because of lack of space.[1]

Even at that early stage of the strike, Militant supporters, as well as expressing total commitment to the miners' struggle, were advocating a programme of action to take the strike forward and give the Left leaders a helping hand. This was in contrast to other groups on the Left, like the CP and the SWP who, despite raising serious criticisms after the strike, acted then as uncritical cheerleaders. In the case of the SWP this was only as an ineffectual group on the sidelines but in the case of the CP, as shown later in this chapter, their role was to be particularly malign.

During the first month of the strike Militant had carried articles on *"a socialist strategy to save the pits"*, which called for the scrapping of interest charges, removing the debt of the NCB and ending competition among nationalised industries; also taking up whether or not a ballot should be called.

Within a week of the strike starting we had shown that miners and union members could not have full confidence in some union leaders when we called for the building of a *"real Triple Alliance at every level."*[2]

We called on the NUM leadership to link in the issue of protecting jobs with action on the national pay claim; this would have drawn in miners even where they did not feel as threatened by the prospect of pit closures.

And throughout the strike we called for a socialist energy plan to save the pits, where coal would be developed as part of an integrated energy plan not dependent on profit or loss balance sheets but on the needs of the workers and society as a whole.[3]

The key tasks for the Left

ONE WEEK into the strike we argued that the key tasks for NUM leaders were to make the strike solid amongst the miners and then take the case against pit closures to the wider working class, calling for all movement of coal stocks and supplies to be brought under effective working-class control. We felt that more needed to be done in properly organising meetings to address non-striking miners.

We made it clear that we did not go along with press and right-wing hypocrisy about calling for a national ballot of the NUM at that stage. That was a matter for the miners and not unelected media barons or High Court judges to decide.

We also struck a warning note about how some picket line clashes between striking and working miners could at some stage hamper the effectiveness of the strike if a way was not found to win over miners in the working areas - whether or not this was to be by a ballot was left open.

Throughout the strike, as well as advocating regular mass meetings for striking miners to keep them informed of the major developments in the strike, Militant also organised regular internal meetings to discuss the complex issues and how the strike could be taken forward. At one meeting in Sheffield in June, over 150 miners from all coalfields attended and discussed strategy and tactics with Peter Taaffe (then editor of Militant and now Socialist Party general secretary) and Brian Ingham (then Militant's industrial correspondent).

Militant supporters had agreed inside our ranks that a ballot about six or seven weeks into the strike would have been a huge unifying factor and would have cut across the propaganda of the right-wing union and Labour leaders.

On a number of occasions, Militant raised the idea of at least a 24-hour general strike being organised in support of the miners.[4] When the South Wales and national NUM funds were threatened with seizure we called for an all-out general strike, such was the seriousness of the threat to the miners and the union movement generally.

At the same time we did not sow any illusions that this would or could be organised by the TUC leaders. Instead, we consistently argued that the NUM leaders should call on the ranks of the union movement to put pressure on their leaders to back the miners with more than words. Again this was not left in an abstract sense. For example, we called on the special NUM national conference on 11-12 July 1984 to name a day for national action in support of the miners.

We added to this a call to rebuild the Triple Alliance from below and demands that union members should put on the Left leaders. At that stage, July 1984, despite the difficulties and obstacles and the likely prospect of a long haul, we said a miners' victory was still there for the taking, particularly as the dock workers had taken solidarity action against scab labour being used on Humberside, which was rapidly spreading. During this action the government threatened to use troops to move coal. We argued that the immediate response of the best trade union leaders, regardless of the inaction of the TUC, should be to call a 24-hour general strike.

Militant's growing strength

WITHOUT DOUBT, if many or all of these demands had been implemented there would have been much more likelihood of the miners winning. But, did Militant, at that stage, have enough influence to ensure these demands were implemented, and what was the response of the Left to these demands?

Militant in 1984 was a very strong, even formidable force in some areas, in the labour movement in Britain. At that stage we were successfully leading the struggle of Liverpool city council.[5] In the unions like civil service union CPSA (forerunner of the PCS) we were leading the Left. At the 1984 CPSA conference over 300 resolutions were tabled criticising the right-wing general secretary of that union Alistair Graham, who was later removed by the Left from the TUC general council.

At the start of the strike there were less than a dozen miners who supported Militant. By the end of the strike this figure had risen to over 500. Our supporters gave the lead in the Broad Left Organising Committee and were the overwhelming majority in the leadership of the Labour Party Young Socialists, which could mobilise 5,000-10,000 of its members for demonstrations in the 1980s.

One of our supporters was a member of Labour's national executive committee (NEC) from the LPYS and was the person who successfully moved at the NEC, seconded by Tony Benn, for a 50p a week levy of Labour Party members to support the miners. Over 30 Constituency Labour Parties regularly elected Militant supporters as delegates to Labour Party conference and two Labour MPs – Dave Nellist in Coventry and Terry Fields in Liverpool – were openly supporters of Militant.

We also had a number of members of trade union national executives but not as many and as much influence as the Socialist Party currently has on union national executives.[6] Although a substantial force and significantly influential we could have only had a decisive impact on the strike if we had had a much stronger position at the base of the unions or members of the NUM national executive and leading supporters as general secretaries or executive members of larger trade unions, which was not the case. But, at all times Militant supporters played an extremely significant role in the strike locally and nationally, practically and politically.

The examples of the practical work done by Militant supporters would fill another book but these examples may help to illustrate the breadth of the work that was involved. There are hundreds of examples in the pages of the Militant.

Militant supporters were among the first to be involved in the setting up and running of miners support groups and committees in the mining areas. Most left-wing groups did not arrive in the coalfields until a few months into the strike. In North Derbyshire, as in other areas, weekly Militant Miner newsletters were produced by striking Militant supporters and handed out on picket lines.

BLOC lobby of the 1984 TUC Conference, Brighton
photo by Militant

But our intervention was not just in the coalfields. In Newham, east London, for example, our supporters organised a meeting of 650 a few weeks after the strike began, with Tony Benn and Liverpool city councillor Derek Hatton speaking.

The LPYS organised hundreds of meetings around the country and participated in the setting up of the Young Miner strike bulletin which was produced throughout the strike. Liverpool council organised hundreds of thousands of pounds of fundraising for the miners. It was Militant that organised the first international visits of miners to win solidarity and raise funds. Miners were helped by Militant to go to South Africa, Australia, the USA, Denmark, Germany, Ireland and many other countries raising thousands of pounds. In workplaces up and down the country Militant supporters organised levies which raised thousands of pounds each month.

The malevolent role of the Communist Party

MILITANT'S FORCES were not sufficient to have altered the course of the strike. Although we had a lot of respect on the Left, not least for the successful struggle in Liverpool and the role of Dave Nellist MP and Terry Fields MP[7], we did not have the ear or influence on the NUM's main leadership nor any of the major trade union leaders. That did not stop us, however, from trying to advance a programme for victory for the miners in every possible way in the unions, Labour Party and society generally.

Particularly in the unions and through BLOC, much was done to try and give the Left leaders a push with helpful pressure from below. One group, though, that did have the ear of the Left union leaders and huge influence inside the NUM was the Communist Party, which at the time claimed 15,000 members – though probably only a few thousand of these were active to any extent.

At that stage the CP was undergoing political turmoil, which eventually caused huge splits. The CP had been moving rightwards for a number of decades and was losing members and influence. One of its allegedly most influential members was Eric Hobsbawm. He was part of a right-wing Eurocommunist faction which argued after Labour's 1983 election defeat that the traditional notions of class struggle and solidarity were a declining force, or indeed at an end, and drew appropriately passive conclusions. These arguments had a marked impact on the politics of what was then called Labour's 'soft left', including Neil Kinnock.

In a number of struggles before the miners' strike, the CP had advocated cross-class or 'popular front' campaigns against the threat of job losses and closures, such as at Ravenscraig steelworks in Scotland.

They had attempted to say that the struggle to keep Ravenscraig open was above class interests but in the national interest. McGahey logically extended this during the strike when he gave in to British Steel management's demand for more coal at Ravenscraig by saying it was *"in the interests of Scotland's industrial future."* [8]

This collaborationist approach resulted in more coal going into the steel plants than was necessary for 'care and maintenance' during the strike.

During the strike some leading CP members, like Bea Campbell, openly lined up with the right wing in advocating a ballot and also argued that mass picketing and solidarity strike action were inappropriate vehicles to win the strike. A leading section of the CP continued to argue for diluting the class nature of the strike by linking up with the churches and pro-capitalist politicians.

According to the Communist Party's industrial organiser of the time: *"What has failed to happen is the bringing together in a mass popular movement of those forces within our society that have already demonstrated sympathy for the miners. This development has been restricted because of a view held that the strike can be won by picketing alone, by the miners alone"* [9]

Nevertheless, the CP, although no longer having as much support on the shopfloor as it had in earlier decades, was still able to count a number of trade union general secretaries amongst its number. Additionally, it exerted an ideological influence at the top of the trade union movement out of all proportion to its real strength on the ground.

Andrew Murray, the chair of the Stop the War Coalition and prominent CP member quotes Ken Gill, a former union general secretary and CP member, on the problems that were then besetting the CP in his recent book on the 'awkward squad': *"The decline of the Communist Party affected the Left, no doubt about it ... Rodney Bickerstaffe* [former leader of public-sector workers union NUPE - a forerunner of today's UNISON] *used to say 'when is the party going to make itself clear'. It was very difficult because the party was practically disowning me then."* [10]

Moreover, the CP had claimed Arthur Scargill as one of its members in the 1950s, as a member of the YCL, and the union's vice-president Mick McGahey was a lifelong CPer. A number of the full-time area officials in Scotland, South Wales and Kent were prominent CP members.

The CP also included Scottish NUM vice-president George Bolton and George Rees, South Wales area secretary. Also, former CPers and Labour Lefts heavily influenced by the CP played a big part in the strike. But none of this alleged influence was used to chart a clear way forward at any stage in the strike.

Desperation of guerrilla tactics

AS MENTIONED, Arthur Scargill's approach was different from the CP in showing an unyielding militancy in defence of the miners. However, even then there were times when his early training in the YCL resurfaced in a rigid and sometimes autocratic approach on issues. This reflected the way the CP had trained up many trade union militants.

Other former CPers like Kim Howells, the South Wales NUM area research officer, played a negative role in the strike from an early stage in terms of statements and practical actions, lacking confidence in the power of the organised working class, which led him to adopt a completely disastrous approach.

After Orgreave, Howells was among the first to denounce mass picketing. Instead, he encouraged small bands of activists to carry out clandestine guerrilla-style activities, which left those miners involved open to danger and prosecution and lowered the consciousness of the miners about the importance of collective mass struggle. This was again opposed by Militant supporters in the South Wales NUM like Philip White and Ian Isaac from St John's.

Howells admitted on a TV documentary in early 2004 of a 'revelation' that had actually been outlined in Seumas Milne's book *The Enemy Within*, ten years earlier.

Howells made great play of the fact that he had never revealed before that after the killing of South Wales taxi driver David Wilkie, who died after miners dropped a slab into the taxi in which he was driving scabs to Merthyr Vale colliery, he went immediately to the South Wales NUM office and destroyed records.

In the documentary he recalls on hearing the death of the taxi driver: *"I thought hang on, we've got all these records we've kept at the NUM offices… we are going to get implicated in this. I remember thinking I've got to get to that office, I've got to destroy everything – and I did. I've never told anybody that before.*

"Howells remembers running to the NUM area office in Pontypridd as soon as he heard the news and 'just getting every bit of picketing information that we had and shredding it' in the expectation of a visit from the police. 'It changed me that moment' he says." [11] Seumas Milne's book goes further about Howells' role, which was quickly followed by a conversion to calling for a return to work.

To this day Howells has never given a full explanation of what it was that caused him so much anxiety at that time, nor has he fully explained how his anticipated inquiries from the police resulted in him becoming the first NUM official to publicly advocate a return to work; a move which was backed by Kinnock and the CP's Eurocommunist faction

The SWP's 'downturn' theory

OTHER GROUPS on the Left, without the same influence as the CP, also proved incapable of either offering a way forward for the strike. Indeed in the case of

Occupation of the South Wales miners' office against attempted sequestration of funds.
Thousands of miners were joined by hundreds of Militants and Labour Party Young Socialists
at very short notice
photo by John Woulfe

the Socialist Workers' Party (SWP) they couldn't comprehend how the strike fitted in with their schematic theory that workers' struggles were in a cycle of downturn after the militancy of the 1970s.

The only prescription that the SWP were able to come up with during the strike was for an escalation of mass picketing, without ever defining what actual numbers of pickets they were talking about and where they would be deployed.

It seems to have escaped their notice that over 10,000 pickets assembled at Orgreave were, unfortunately, unsuccessful. Whilst not abandoning the weapon of the mass picket as a result of that defeat, it was clear that there needed to be a better suggestion than repeating the mantra of first world war generals of just dragooning more troops out of the trenches.

In their book reviewing the strike they conclude: *"Throughout the coalfields the mass picketing strategy which brought victory in 1972 hadn't failed – it had not been seriously tried."* They recognised that solidarity action was also needed but argued that *"the precondition of that action was consistent and vigorous picketing by the miners themselves. The miners could not expect to win the support of other workers unless they were seen themselves to picket massively."* [12]

Equally, the SWP's peculiar theoretical construct of the downturn (flying in the face of the increased militancy of other struggles at the same time as the miners and the mass mobilisations in support of Militant-led Liverpool city council) did not really countenance the possibility of that happening.

From this theory they were capable of drawing all the wrong negative conclusions in the space of one paragraph such as this: *"One might say the strike itself clearly revealed the scale of the downturn in the class struggle – in, for example, the willingess of miners and other workers to cross NUM picket lines. The trade union leaders could hardly substitute themselves for a passive and divided rank-and-file. The weakness of workplace organisation was undoubtedly one of the decisive features of the strike."* [13]

Although they waxed lyrical about how the *"activists who supported the miners could have been crystallised into a powerful movement for class-struggle methods"* [14] they did not concretely ever say how their aims of mass picketing or this class-struggle method could be delivered in the context of the alleged *"weakness of workplace organisation."* This meant in reality they practised a limited participation in the support groups in the big cities - and played an insignificant part in any of the support groups in the mining areas. They had no participation or impact on any of the major debates amongst the miners in the NUM itself.

Indeed, as has been evidenced on other occasions, such a huge movement of the working class saw them floundering and incapable of playing any effective role.

Preparing for future battles

MILITANT, ALONE among the groups on the Left, was the only trend to make significant gains out of the miners' strike. Unfortunately because of the huge blow of the defeat and the political effect it had, many miners and their families who joined us in 1984-85 dropped out of political activity later on, although a number have since come back into the ranks of the Socialist Party.

Overall, Militant took a huge surge forward during the events of 1984-85 leaving us well placed numerically and organisationally for the battles ahead in Liverpool and over the poll tax, despite the objective difficulties that we would face because of the miners' defeat after the betrayal of the right-wing union and Labour leaders.

NOTES

1   From *Militant* issue 693, 30 March 1984

2   *Militant* issue 690

3   See *Militant* issue 693

4   For example even as early as *Militant* issue 696, 20 April 1984.

5   For a full account of this struggle see *Liverpool A City That Dared to Fight* by Peter Taaffe and Tony Mulhearn, Fortress Books 1987

6   For a fuller account of the strength and role of Militant during the 1980s see *The Rise of Militant* by Peter Taaffe, Socialist Books, 1994

7   Arthur Scargill, for instance, spoke at an election rally for Terry Fields in 1983

8   Quoted in *The Great Strike*, Callinicos and Simons, Socialist Worker publication, 1985

9   Marxism Today, March 1985

10 *A New Labour Nightmare – the rise of the awkward squad*, Andrew Murray, Verso Books 2003

11 *The Enemy Within*, Seumas Milne, Verso 1994, p203

12 ibid page 234

13 *The Great Strike*, Callinicos and Simons, Socialist Workers' Party, London 1985, p235

14 ibid

Coal Board chairman MacGregor gets some unexpected advice

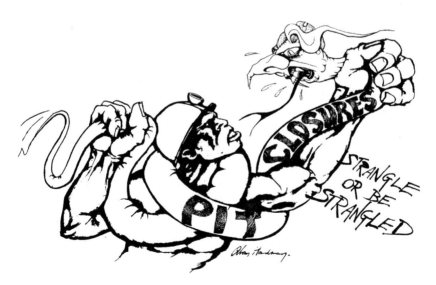

STRANGLE
OR BE
STRANGLED

THE MINERS came closer to victory than they could scarcely have realised in October-November 1984. A number of memoirs, including from Thatcher and MacGregor themselves, subsequently confirmed this.

Thatcher recalled the danger she faced at the time of the threatened NACODS strike, when hardline NCB bosses MacGregor and Cowans had insisted that NACODS members had to cross picket lines and go into work, even if a pit was solidly on strike. This incensed the moderate NACODS leaders who were under great pressure from their rank and file who clearly wanted to do more for the miners than sit at home waiting for the strike to end.

A ballot of NACODS members saw them deliver an 82.5% yes to strike action and a series of NCB miscalculations and incompetence threatened to bring out the NACODS members, which would have stopped every pit in the country working, including in Nottinghamshire.

As one government insider said: *"A bandwagon might begin to roll in Mr Scargill's favour."* Nine years later, Thatcher described this crisis period for her government: *"We had got so far and we were in danger of losing everything because of a silly mistake. We had to make it quite clear that if it was not cured immediately then the actual management of the Coal Board could indeed have brought down the government. The future of the government at that moment was in their hands and they had to remedy their terrible mistake."* [1]

Again, ten years later, Frank Ledger, the Central Electricity Generating Board's director of operations, recounted how they had only planned for a six-month strike and that the situation at this time was verging on the *"catastrophic"*. [2]

Militant suporter Jon Dale visited Ratcliffe power station, near Nottingham, a few years after the strike. An engineer told him how, in October 1984, their coal stockpile looked as big as ever from the road. But behind, it had all gone. Small emergency diesel generators were being run flat out around the clock, while the main coal-fired generators were just run for peak demand.

Ultimately, the key factor that defeated the miners was not their lack of militant, even revolutionary spirit in the face of the most sustained vicious state onslaught on them and their families; nor was it lack of support from the wider ranks of the working class. And it was not the mistakes that the leaders of the NUM made at national and area level – although some of these were of significant importance later in the strike.

The absolutely crucial factor in the ultimate defeat of the strike was the treacherous and cowardly role of the trade union and Labour leaders. But even without their support the miners came closer to defeating Thatcher than they knew.

From an early stage, right-wing leaders inside the unions were playing a consciously strikebreaking role. Initially this was done more secretively and underhandedly than was to be the case later on in the strike.

This conscious sabotage can be difficult to overcome, given the dead hand these so-called leaders can lay upon the workers' movement. But it is not impossible that even the most entrenched of these right-wing leaders can be overturned and removed as has been shown in unions like Amicus and the PCS.

In 1984 they represented a conscious strikebreaking force playing on the fears and prejudices of the most backward section of workers. The 'new realists' played on the idea that nothing could be done to stop Thatcherism and the only option left was to submit and accept privatisation, anti-union laws and the onslaught of neo-liberalism – described as Reaganism and Thatcherism in those days.

They passively accepted the ruling class's right to manage and run society, which meant riding roughshod over all the gains the working class had made through their trade unions in the previous two centuries.

This certainly did not inspire workers with much confidence and was not fought against by most of the Left trade union leaders. They lacked confidence in the working class and mistakenly blamed them for the crimes and defeats of Thatcherism.

Snatching defeat from the jaws of victory

TONY BENN recalls in his diaries that, while the wider working class was rallying in support of the miners, the Left union leaders had begun squabbling about how to support the miners from 1 April onwards, less than a month into the strike.

The Left leaders had become accustomed to leading shorter, sharper strikes in a relatively easier period and were in no way prepared for the big battles of the 1980s against a more determined, brutal ruling class.

Their inability to lead a resistance and their failure to mobilise against the biggest threat and challenge faced by the trade union movement since the 1920s squandered nearly all that had been built up by workers in the intervening decades.

The Left union leaders had been conditioned in an era where they could gain concessions by negotiation and compromise – particularly over pay and conditions. With the growing strength of the trade union movement in the 1950s and 1960s, its influence reached a point in Britain that many had not believed possible. This union density in the working population and workers' influence over their jobs had mainly arisen in a gradual way from the prolonged economic upswing after the second world war.

Whilst there were the big set-piece struggles and strikes it was predominantly the prolonged economic boom that gave workers confidence to demand more and to

Just a few of the many Militant Miner bulletins and related material produced at the time

threaten action if the management didn't give it. In the 1950s and 1960s the strategy and tactics of union leaders became a process of negotiation and compromise with management, using the threat of calling the workers out if management tried it on too much.

Militant made the points many times in that period that Britain's bosses were buying industrial peace at the cost of future economic and social ruin for the capitalists.

This was a period of continued economic decline for British capitalism, which inevitably would lead to bitter clashes between bosses and workers as the capitalists attempted to increase their profitability by reducing the share of wealth going to the working class.

During the 1970s – particularly after the simultaneous world economic downturn of 1974-75 –the capitalist class began to attack workers' conditions won in the post-war period; both on the shopfloor and the social gains won through the welfare state.

The struggles of the early 1970s – particularly the miners' strikes of 1972 and 74 – exerted elements of workers' control over management decisions unsurpassed since. But later in the 1970s, the tactics that had proved effective earlier, such as mass picketing and secondary, solidarity action, were being put more to the test and winning fewer victories.

Grunwick – the two-year-long struggle for union recognition of predominantly Asian women workers, despite mass pickets of tens of thousands, including the presence of right-wing Labour cabinet ministers - was ultimately defeated.

Similarly, the so-called 'winter of discontent', was a formidable show of strength from union members dissatisfied with the Labour government's wage freeze policies and their union leaders' accommodation with it. Nevertheless, the right-wing Labour leaders disingenuously blamed the union members' justified strike action for the defeat of the deeply unpopular 1974-1979 Labour government and of bringing in Thatcherism. This criticism sent the Left union leaders into retreat.

Thatcherism had been ushered in precisely by that Labour government when it carried through huge cuts in public expenditure at the behest of the International Monetary Fund, which gave the Labour government a financial bail-out package in the economic crisis of 1976 provided the government carried out IMF-dictated austerity measures.

Thatcher's election in 1979 was to usher in an era of class battles not seen since the 1920s as British capitalism attempted to recover its 'right' to hire and fire free from any union influence. Thatcher and her cabinet were, however, not as powerful as the history books portray.

Their ultimate success in beating the miners to usher in a reign of economic and social terror, was only achieved with the class collaboration of the right-wing union leaders and the inability of the Left leaders to use the latent power of the working class.

Should Scargill have settled?

GIVEN THE clear inability of the Left union leaders to deliver the sort of solidarity action needed and to take on Thatcher, was there any other course open to the miners? Should they have avoided struggle at that time and perhaps waited for a better period? Was it possible if they had accepted the NCB's definition of pit closures in July 1984 that such a strategic retreat would have left them in a better position to temporarily slow down the pit closure programme, deprive Thatcher of her 'industrial Falklands' and live to fight another day? Should they have settled on the same terms as NACODS did in November – as Arthur Scargill suggested he was prepared to in January 1985?

The evidence from other industries at the time was that the so-called tactical flair of the right-wing union leaders, such as in steel, or compromise deals of Left leaders fared no better, with tens of thousands of jobs lost.

Clearly, at certain stages of the dispute the personal character of Thatcher, MacGregor and Scargill played a large part in whether or not there could have been a settlement.

But, as was shown subsequently, once the balance of class forces had shifted in their favour, Thatcher and the Tories were out to destroy the mining industry and the mining unions. After the strike they arrogantly tossed aside the NACODS' deal negotiated in October, leading the NACODS leaders to threaten another strike.

Thatcher particularly made it clear that she was not prepared to settle on any terms and intervened at key points later in the dispute to scupper any prospect of the NCB negotiating a deal behind her back. Inevitably, even if the miners had suffered a partial defeat this would not have been enough for her.

She made it clear that the miners – like the Liverpool councillors – *"had no respect for her position"* and wanted them crushed to show that militancy would not pay. Towards the end of the strike when it became clearer that they were likely to win, the Tories wanted to use Scargill as a latter-day Braveheart like William Wallace, as an example to others who dared to take on Thatcher: *"As one government minister observed: 'Our leader will not be satisfied until Scargill is seen trotting round Finchley tethered to the back of the prime ministerial Jaguar.'"* [Finchley was Thatcher's parliamentary constituency] [3]

Thatcher clearly understood she was fighting a battle for the whole of the ruling class to neuter the trade unions, to remove socialist influence from the Labour Party and to re-establish management's right to manage and to hire and fire in the workplace. Unfortunately, none of the Left leaders, with the exception of Arthur Scargill, saw it in such clear class terms.

Although the memoirs of her government ministers tend to over-emphasise a high degree of unity against making concessions to the miners – as opposed to the splits over concessions they made to Liverpool council. However, this probably reflected their confidence in the preparation that the Tory government had made for a miners' strike, the fact that the timidity of the Labour leadership and the majority of the trade union leaders posed them no serious problems during the dispute and that no serious, sustained second front opened up at any stage. If the dockers or NACODS had come out for a longer period or if a 24-hour general strike had materialised, then it is more likely that cracks would have opened up in Thatcher's government.

However, there were serious splits and wobbles within the NCB and between MacGregor and Tory energy secretary Peter Walker. Many NCB officials and managers were initially opposed to the hard line being foisted on them by the government and later on, at certain key stages, ineptitude and tactical blunders caused huge rifts inside the NCB. At one stage, MacGregor was effectively removed as the front man for the coal board.

Cracks open in the NUM

INSIDE THE NUM there was a high degree of unity in the areas where the strike was solid at the start of the strike. The right wing in the union, whilst disagreeing with Scargill and the Left's tactics, would not have dared venture opposition to the strike such was the strength of feeling against the Tory pit closure programme.

However, at local level as the strike wore on, a number of serious splits opened up, particularly after Orgreave and the back-to-work movement developed. At the same time, what has been clearly revealed by Seumas Milne and others is that the state's security services were hard at work inside the NUM doing their utmost to undermine and discredit the miners' struggles.

However, all the efforts of the state, including extensive phone tapping and the use of agents provocateurs like Roger Windsor, who was the chief executive of the NUM during the strike, would not have resulted in the defeat of the miners or been able to take advantage of weakness or splits inside the union if the struggle had been going forward.

Clearly, from September onwards there was a leading layer in the NUM, with Kim Howells and Terry Thomas from the South Wales NUM, along with McGahey in

Scotland, who were looking for a settlement. Scargill, sensing more accurately the mood of the rank-and-file miners against any sell out, was opposed to settling in the marathon negotiations that took place that month, that looked close to coming to a deal accepting the coal board's definition of when a pit should be closed.

Correctly, he realised that in the use of the words *"where a pit cannot be benefi-cially developed"* the coal board wanted to add was a catch-all clause that would give them carte blanche to close a pit. Under the Plan for Coal a pit would only be closed if all reserves had been exhausted or if it was geologically unsafe. Even the *Times* editorialised at the time that beneficially *"is not an innocent word. It symbol-ises the division between two philosophies."*

Even the *Sunday Times* Insight team recognised the obstacles being thrown in the NUM's path: *"While it was easily the best offer made to Scargill in the course of the dispute, it is important to recognise that it would still have represented a retreat."* [4]

Had the new wording been accepted then not only would the majority of striking miners have seen it as a sell-out but inevitably it would have meant that the NUM would have been drawn into another large-scale confrontation with the NCB and government sooner rather than later. Or, it would have seen widespread localised struggles against pit closures, where pits would have been sliced off salami style without any possibility of a national or even area fightback being mounted.

This was certainly what happened after the miners returned to work in March 1985. The exhaustion of the year-long battle meant there was little energy and resources left to mount an effective fight, even though the best activists tried valiantly to stop pit closures using argument and mobilising local communities – but the threat of strike action by the national NUM was a spent force.

It is possible that the NUM may have been in a state of less exhaustion and weakness if it had beat a strategic retreat in July, September or October 1984, which may have left it slightly stronger to fight future battles. However, without the ability to bring in other unions behind their struggle it is difficult to see if they could progress any further forward against stopping pit closures. In July, it was a clear a second front was opening up as the dockers took strike action.

At the same time, it is likely that a majority of NUM members would have reject-ed a return to work on those conditions, holding out and hoping - as Arthur Scargill described it - for "General Winter" to come to their aid.

Wounded but not slain

IN THE winter of 1984-85, the miners came close to bringing about the elusive power cuts, which could have caused enormous problems for the Tory govern-ment. Unfortunately, by then they were running out of money (intensified by the

seizure of the union's assets, which were handed from an undemocratically appointed judge to an undemocratically appointed auditor), unable to step up the picketing that was needed at the power plants. The leadership of the union was exhausted of ideas – apart from holding on – to step up the action needed. Even then, it still required efforts to get to the rank-and-file power workers below their rotten right-wing leadership (who were more than happy to see the NUM hung out to dry).

For instance: *"At St John's colliery in Mid-Glamorgan, the 33-year-old lodge secretary Ian Isaac, had made his own clear-eyed assessment, as the funds diminished and the effectiveness of the pickets, never overwhelming, steadily ebbed away. A Militant supporter, who had written his diploma thesis at Ruskin College, Oxford, on the fabled radicalism of his home town, Maesteg, his whole philosophy revolved around a belief in the power of the well-organised worker, but he had looked at the signs this time and drawn his own conclusions: 'The strike was all done on a haphazard basis. We should have billeted our men in towns where power workers live and really worked at getting to know them and convincing them. We reached the stage where we didn't even have the money to travel to see the power station people. By November we were logistically beaten'."* [5]

By then the Left leaders had adopted an air of passive resignation, at best stepping up the financial and personal assistance to miners and their families but unable or incapable of providing any display of working-class action against the increasingly sharp Tory offensive.

As the winter dragged on and Christmas approached the working class of Britain and internationally showed the most marvellous solidarity with the miners. Hundreds of thousands of pounds were raised and gifts of food and toys for the children came from every continent of the earth.

Although these were very difficult times for the miners and their families very few gave up. In many ways, as many have said since in documentaries and books, the adversity reawakened the solidarity and comradeship of mining communities and with the wider working class.

Anyone who lived through it will never forget that year. In one year, miners, their wives, families, supporters, trade unionists, socialists and Marxists in the Militant tendency learnt more about the role of the state and the need to change the unions and workers' parties into fighting bodies than could be learned in a thousand books of theory – as important as understanding theory is in seeing it as a guide to action in major working-class struggles.

Had the miners achieved a historic victory against the odds, then with such lessons being learned this would have ushered in a huge sweeping move to the Left inside the workers' organisations and in society generally.

Their defeat instead steered in a period of new realism, social partnership and sweetheart deals, which the union movement is only beginning to slowly overcome. But the lessons are there for a new generation to learn from as increased working-class consciousness and confidence removes the scars of the miners' defeat.

NOTES

1   *The Enemy Within*, Seumas Milne, Verso, London 1994, p17

2   ibid, p16

3   Hugo Young, *One of Us*, London Pan Books edition 1993, p376

4   *Strike, 358 days that shook the nation*, Sunday Times Insight team, Coronet 1985, p137

5   ibid p232

A cartoon from 1992 when Michael Heseltine announced more widespread closures in the Coal industry - producing a huge outcry

THE MINERS' defeat saw them marching back defiantly behind their banners. Although they were unable to stand up once again to the accelerated pit closure programme, a war of attrition between management and unions took place in many coalfields.

A campaign was also launched to get the hundreds of sacked miners reinstated. Even to this day the victimisation of miners continues, sometimes in the most unexpected ways. In February 2003, ex-NUM official, 69-year-old Jock Glen from east Scotland, was summoned to attend a meeting at the US consulate in London over his request for a visa to enter the USA on a family holiday because he was arrested during the miners' strike 20 years ago.

In some mining communities the scars of division still remain. Ian Whyles, a North Derbyshire striking miner and Militant supporter, now a Socialist Party member, has barely spoken to his son since the strike ended. His son returned to work halfway through the year-long strike. Even then, Ian *"went to speak to him and told him he was old enough to do what he wanted to do. But I reminded him that he had to remember the strike would one day come to an end, but that the community would still be here"*… but the real turning point came when *"I saw him with a UDM badge on* [the Union of Democratic Mineworkers – the breakaway scab union in Nottingham] *and that's when we really fell out."* [1]

A battle is over but the war continues

MANY AREAS only reluctantly went back to work; incensed at the Tory government and angry and bitter at the Labour and trade union leaders who let them down. The acceleration of the pit-closure programme led to a social blitzkrieg in many of the former mining communities, where drug addiction, chronic long-term unemployment, poverty, crime and other devastating social problems became rife. Eventually Thatcherism went rampant after the defeat of the miners but strong echoes of the miners' strike were to resonate in other big struggles during the Thatcher years: such as the Wapping printers' dispute; the P&O strikers and most notably in the poll tax struggle, led by Militant supporters, which ultimately led to Thatcher's downfall.

Dizzy with her own success, however, Thatcher presided over a policy of massive deindustrialisation of British industry and further impoverishment of significant sections of working class and middle-class people. Thatcher thought the benefits accruing to the British economy from North Sea oil would sufficiently offset the loss of manufacturing industry. But, even immediately after the strike, Tory ministers were privately fuming at how little gratitude was shown towards them for defeating the miners:

"For months after the strike was over, ministers often alluded in conversation to the strange ingratitude of the British public... When the strike ended there was no full-throated roar of approval of the kind which had been heard, almost universally, when the Argentineans surrendered in Port Stanley." [2]

Whilst Thatcher and her acolytes would have preferred the approval, nevertheless, as Hugo Young observed: *"The truth was that however muddy the surface waters, the deeper currents flowing out of the miners' strike carried her in the directions she wanted to go."* [3]

Witch-hunt against the miners and Militant

LABOUR LEADER Neil Kinnock also found the flowing of this tide to his advantage in intensifying the witch-hunt inside the Labour Party against the miners' leader Arthur Scargill, against the Militant-led Liverpool city council leaders and against Militant supporters inside the Labour Party.

Kinnock, contrary to convention, spoke twice at the Labour Party conference in Bournemouth in 1985 – each time to attack the Left. Firstly he used his main conference speech to attack Scargill indirectly and Liverpool city council head on. Then he replied to a debate on the miners' strike to attack Scargill and rule out any retrospective legislation to reinstate or support victimised miners.

To Kinnock and his cronies this was all part of the campaign to root out militancy and 'modernise' the Labour Party – a codeword for accepting the free-market policies of Thatcherism. This began the process of transforming Labour into an openly pro-capitalist party, like the Democrats in the USA, which has led to the 'Thatcherism with a grin' of Blair today.

However, Kinnock's rapid shift to the right did him no favours on the British electoral field. Despite claiming that militancy was an electoral liability – flying in the face of the evidence of Labour being 5% ahead of the Tories during the miners' strike and the growing support for Labour in Liverpool – Kinnock and his modernisers like Peter Mandelson, Charles Clarke and Patricia Hewitt went on to spectacularly lose both the 1987 and 1992 elections.

Had the miners won in 1984-85 then it could have seen Thatcher weakened and possibly removed from office, with a Tory defeat at the subsequent general election. The defeat of the Tories was something Kinnock never achieved for all his spin and slick presentation – it took the mass movement of the anti-poll tax struggle, led by Militant, to get rid of Thatcher.

As the effects of the 1980s economic boom wore on, Labour had to wait until 1997 to return to office. The less than inspiring Tony Blair won a landslide (in seats but not in votes) due to the amazing hatred that had built up for the rampant, corrupt, and sleazy Tories over the intervening 12 years. The effects of the miners' defeat rang loudest in the official corridors of the trade union movement. After the miners' strike the union leaders began a rightward march that was only halted a few years ago with the election of the 'awkward squad'.

This class-conciliationist mood at the top did not reflect the growing anger of the rank and file of the trade union movement or the wider working class generally.

Certainly, until the end of the 1980s, although there was a weakening of union structures and a (justified) lack of confidence that the union leaders would mount effective action in defence of union members, the defeat of the miners did not result in a spontaneous big bang that smashed the trade unions.

The trade unions were never completely smashed, as Thatcher had hoped for, despite the craven cowardice and betrayals of the right-wing union leaders. More correctly, there was a gradual corrosion of union structures and a continued deterioration in confidence in the right-wing union leaders.

Even the huge ideological impact the collapse of Stalinism had in the 1990s did not result in the end of trade unionism or socialist ideas, as we have seen with the resurgence of both in recent years. Rather, the effects of the 1990s were a throwing back of consciousness on political and trade union ideology; including a weakening of belief in the solidarity of workers taking collective action. On a number of occasions big struggles broke out against employers taking the cosh to their workforce. In general, these were more localised struggles (although they did attain a certain national significance, like the Liverpool Dockers' strike in the 1990s) but not so much the idea of trade unions taking effective national industrial action.

Social devastation of mining communities

FOR THE miners and their families, however, the result of the strike's defeat has been devastating in many areas. Yet, despite that, most of the miners who stood out for the whole 12 months of the strike would not change anything about what they did. This applies also to the miners' wives who became politicised during the strike and have never looked back.

Dave Nixon, a 27-year-old miner in 1984, looking back at the strike in a BBC2 documentary in 2004 summed up how many miners recall the mixture of sadness and pride they still feel: *"Following the colliery band we marched back to the pit through the community we fought for, not with our heads held high but bowed low in sorrow. I remember clearly the pride, elation, bravery, fear, sadness and sorrow; every emotion that one would expect to experience in a lifetime, brought together during the 12-month strike and looking back I truly say, no regrets."*

The tens of thousands of ordinary miners who stuck out for the whole 12 months can feel pride and will be an inspiration to future generations looking for examples of workers' willingness to struggle. It was not through lack of determination or fighting spirit on the part of these miners and their families and supporters that their struggle was defeated.

The example that these miners had given led to a huge public outcry in 1992 against Tory cabinet minister Heseltine's proposals for a massive further cut in deep-mined coal and the loss of over 30,000 mining jobs.

A tidal surge of anger swelled up when all the miners' predictions about what the Tories were prepared to do to their industry was graphically borne out. Massive demonstrations took place in London, where all sections of the population came out in support. Combined with their support for the miners came a growing hatred of the Tories after the economic debacle of Black Wednesday[4] and the anger at the corruption and sleaziness of the Tories which was then starting to unfold.

A National Union of Teachers rep at Holland Park school, west London, recalls how teachers came out at his school in support of the miners: *"The NUT group at my secondary school voted to take half-day strike action so that we could join the march through west London - all completely outside of the anti-trade union laws, of course. I believe some schools in Camden also took action that day.*

"Our group of teachers and students made the short walk through the side streets and joined up in Kensington Church Street. There was an incredible crescendo of noise as we came out into the main body of the march. From all points around, from shop doorways, windows and balconies, hundreds and hundreds of shop workers, bank staff, waiters from the restaurants, ordinary shoppers and residents were shouting their support. Many had improvised banners and placards against the pit closures. It was the same in Kensington High Street. It was almost unbelievable, like a huge outpouring of support, from workers primarily, but also from many who could not be classified as working class by any stretch of the imagination. After all these were some of the richest streets in Britain, and hundreds of miles from any pit. It's where the upper class shop, eat and live. Maybe, some of it was guilt because it was now clear that what the miners had said all along was now being proved true; but I think it was more than that."[5]

Arthur Scargill correctly called for the TUC to call a 24-hour general strike in support of the miners and there's little doubt that the public mood would have supported the action against the increasingly despised Tories, who had just narrowly won the 1992 election against Kinnock. However, he also spoke on platforms with CBI representatives, echoing the 'broad alliance' policy that the CP had advocated in 1984-85.

Again the TUC did nothing concrete but desperately pleaded with government ministers. The fact that Heseltine did a body swerve (reminiscent of Thatcher in 1981) owed everything to the growing mood of public anger and nothing to the inaction of the TUC.

The respite against pit closures was only temporary. And under Blair's New Labour government the continued rundown of the coal industry has continued apace. Within a few months of its election in 1997 a secret report was leaked to the Independent newspaper revealing that Labour planned to let RJB Mining destroy 5,000 mining jobs (RJB was the privatised successor to British Coal which later became UK Coal). In July 2002 came the announcement that the Selby super-pit complex, which had only opened 20 years previously and was heralded as the future of mining, was to close with the loss of 2,000 jobs. Again the refrain was that *"deteriorating geological conditions and continuing financial losses"* meant the pit had no prospect of *"becoming viable".*

In 2003 the UK coal industry employed just over 9,000 people – approximately 6,500 of those in deep mines in only 12 pits; the other 2,500 are employed in 49 opencast sites. In 2002-2003 total UK coal production was 28.9 million tonnes, of which 15.8 million came from deep mines – overall this was a fall of 13% in coal production from the previous year and is less than 18% of what was produced 20 years ago. The UK imported almost as much coal as it produced in 2003 - 28.6 million tonnes, although this was down from the record figure of 35.3 million tonnes in 2001 – a sure sign that many more pits could and should have been kept open, even by the logic of capitalist economics.

Ironically, there has been an increase in demand for coal for electricity generation in the last few years because of the increasing costs of oil and gas as supplies become scarcer. If ever there was an example of the short-sightedness of British capitalism – particularly Thatcher and her conscious decision to deindustrialise Britain to weaken the working class and the trade unions – then the run down of coal is the prime example.

Unbending and unbreakable

ALL OF the miners' opponents have suffered ignominy in one form or another. Thatcher was ousted after the debacle of the poll tax; Kinnock never won a ballot in the form of a general election and went on to be a European Commissioner on a millionaire lifestyle, frequently under attack from allegations of corruption in the EU section he presides over; MacGregor left the NCB under a cloud and died in 1998 and Robert Maxwell, the Daily Mirror owner who accused Scargill of corruption mysteriously fell off his boat and drowned when his attempts to corruptly swindle the Mirror workers out of their pension rights came to light. The UDM has dwindled as a discredited force inside the declining coalfields. It has recently been involved in scandals, accused of arranging lucrative deals from miners' compensation, which has allowed UDM leaders to earn salaries and bonuses of at least £150,000 a year.

All of the union leaders who undermined the miners' struggle have all gone and will in no way be remembered in contrast to Arthur Scargill. His predictions about the butchery of the coal industry during the strike and the need to struggle were proved presciently true.

He made mistakes during the dispute. And although he was correct to break from Labour in 1997 he made some fundamental political mistakes over the way his Socialist Labour Party was launched and run. However, whatever mistakes he made during the strike, no one could deny his refusal to buckle under the Tories and class enemy's pressure. He stood firm during the strike, an inspiration to the striking miners themselves, and has never renounced the conduct of the strike or seen it as anything less than justified.

Although he is an isolated figure on the fringes of the Left today, the example he gave during the strike still resonates. It was no accident that the first 'insult' the Labour government reached for in trying to denigrate the firefighters during their dispute in 2002-2003 was accusing the union's members of being *"Scargillites"*.

Whilst the Socialist Party would have disagreements with Scargill on this or that strategic or tactical decision during the strike, we believe that identifying strikers today with the heroic example of the miners in 1984-85 will come to be worn as a badge of pride amongst workers involved in new struggles. It will be seen as an example of being willing to go to the end in defending the interests of the working class. But, as Militant said at the end of the strike in 1985: *"Scargill did prove to be 'unbreakable' but an unbending will by itself is insufficient."* [6]

The legacy for today

THE MINERS' strike of 1984-85 is rich in lessons about the determination of working-class people to struggle. But it is also rich in lessons about the strategy and tactics that trade unionists need to apply.

It also shows the need for a wider political understanding in working-class organisations about the need to assess the possibilities of success of a strike, the options available, the balance of class forces, as well as surveying the stage of development of the trade unions and workers' organisations. Arising from that comes the need to transform and retransform the workers' organisations into militant class-struggle bodies with mass involvement of the rank and file, linked to a leadership armed with a clear Marxist understanding and programme to change society. The magnificent firefighters' and postal workers' actions in 2003, despite the timidity of their official leaders, showed a new willingness to struggle and a refusal to be intimidated by threats and anti-union laws.

Today's generation and future generations in Britain will increasingly look to change their unions into fighting organisations. They will look back on the British miners' strike of 1984-1985 and seek to learn the many lessons from that heroic struggle of how best to effectively challenge capitalism and replace it with a new, socialist society.

Building a movement to achieve these goals would be the best way to honour and avenge the defeated miners who fought so valiantly in the 1984-1985 Great Strike for jobs.

We believe young workers will increasingly look to the ideas of the Socialist Party and Marxism and advocate our programme for changing the unions and society, including the following demands:

- For the unions to take immediate action to implement their current minimum wage demands, as a step towards a legal minimum of £8 an hour. No exemptions
- For an annual increase in the minimum wage, linked to average earnings. For a minimum income of £320 a week
- A range of policies to achieve full employment including the introduction of a maximum 35-hour week without loss of pay
- Employment protection rights for all from day one of employment
- Reject Welfare to Work; for the right to decent benefits, training or a job without compulsion
- Scrap the anti-union laws
- Trade unions to be democratically controlled by members
- Full-time officials should be regularly elected and receive the average wage of the workers they represent
- Renationalise the privatised utilities under democratic working-class control and management
- Major investment into a integrated system of energy production that meets the needs of the people and the environment
- A plan of sustainable energy production, including an environmentally friendly use of coal, to be drawn up between energy workers, trade unions and representatives of society generally
- For massive investment into the development of sustainable energy resources - including solar, wind and wave power - in order to reduce fossil fuel use
- For the urgent phasing out of all nuclear power, with guaranteed, well-paid,

alternative employment for the workforce

● A massive increase of public spending into healthcare, housing, education, childcare, leisure and community facilities

● Take into public ownership the top 150 big companies, banks and building societies that dominate the economy under democratic working-class control and management, with compensation paid only on the basis of proven need

● An end to the rule of profit

● Campaign to form a new mass party of the working class.

● For a socialist plan of production

● For a socialist society and economy run to meet the needs of all whilst protecting our environment

NOTES

1 *Worksop Guardian*, 13 February 2004

2 Hugo Young, *One of Us*, Pan edition, London 1993 p375

3 Ibid, p377

4 On this day, 16 September 1992, interest rates were increased twice in one day to a record 15% to vainly try and keep Britain in the European Exchange Rate Mechanism (ERM) after huge speculation against the pound. It was seen as one of the most spectacular failures of economic policy by a British government.

5 Interview with Bob Sulatycki. Many other examples that illustrate this movement were also carried in *Militant* at the time

6 *Militant*, issue 739, 8 March 1985

Bibliography

The Miners' Strike 1984-85 – a bibliography

Unfortunately, some of these books are now out of print,
but should still be available from lending libraries or secondhand

- *Miners 1984-94, A Decade of Endurance,* Joe Owens, Polygon, Edinburgh 1994
- *Digging Deeper,* Huw Benyon (editor) London 1985
- *Strike, 358 Days that Shook the Nation,* Sunday Times Insight team, Coronet 1985.
- *The Enemies Within,* Ian MacGregor with Rodney Tyler, Fontana 1985
- *Scargill the Unauthorised Biography,* Paul Routledge, Harper Collins 1993
- *The Communist Party of Great Britain since 1920,* James Eadie and David Renton. Palgrave publishers, 2002)
- *Militant* and *Militant International Review* 1984-85
- *The Rise of Militant,* Peter Taaffe, Militant Publications, London 1994
- *Liverpool the City that Dared to Fight,* Tony Mulhearn and Peter Taaffe, Fortress books, London 1988
- *One of Us,* Hugo Young, Pan Books edition, London 1993
- *The Enemy Within,* Seumas Milne, Verso, London 1994
- *The Great Strike,* Alex Callinicos and Mike Simons, Socialist Workers' Party, London 1985
- *Strikes and the Media,* Nicholas Jones, Blackwell, Oxford 1986
- *Policing the Miners' Strike,* edited by Bob Fine and Robert Millar, Cobden, London 1985
- Geoffrey Goodman, *The Miners' Strike,* Pluto, London 1985
- *The Miners' Strike, 1984-85: Loss without Limit,* Martin Adeney, Routledge and Keegan Paul, London, 1986
- David Jones, *Media hits the pits, the media and the coal dispute.* Campaign for Press and Broadcasting Freedom, 1985
- *The Battle for Orgreave,* Bernard Jackson, Vanson Wardle, Brighton 1986

socialist books

Some of the books listed above may also be available from Socialist Books.
To order further copies of this publication or any from either the list overleaf or
other publications published by Socialist Books contact us at:

Socialist Books, PO Box 24697, London E11 1YD
telephone: 020 8988 8789 or **email: socialistbooks@socialistparty.org.uk**
or online at the socialist party **website: www.socialistparty.org.uk**

other titles available from socialist books

- **Empire Defeated - Vietnam War: the lessons for today**
  by Peter Taaffe
  Published February 2004. 128 pages paperback
  A history of the Vietnam War drawing out the lessons to be learnt from this conflict, especially in the aftermath of the Iraq war. Price £6.00

- **Socialism in the 21st Century: the way forward for anti-capitalism**
  by Hannah Sell
  Published August 2002. 90 pages paperback
  An essential read for anti-capitalists, trade union activists and socialists. Price £5.00

- **The Rise of Militant: Militant's 30 years** by Peter Taaffe
  Published 1995. 570 pages paperback
  Story of Militant, forerunner of the Socialist Party, from its birth. Price £10.99

- **Liverpool - A city that Dared to Fight** by Tony Mulhearn and Peter Taaffe
  Published 1988, 500 pages paperback
  Militant led Liverpool city council's battle against the Thatcher government 1983-1997. Price £7.95

- **Cuba: Socialism and democracy Debates on the Revolution and Cuba Today**
  by Peter Taaffe
  Published 2000. 120 pages paperback
  Defence of the Socialist Party's analysis of the Cuban revolution. Price £5.00

- **France 1968: Month of Revolution Lessons of the General Strike**
  by Clare Doyle
  Published 1988, 80 pages paperback
  Ten million French workers on strike, many occupying their factories. Eyewitness account. Price £4.00